PLAGUE OVER E

"... a witty social panorama of tl
... what makes this an engrossing play is (his) expert recreation of an unlovely period in English life." Michael Billington, *Guardian*

"With great aplomb de Jongh's play whisks us from courtroom to gay club, from the heart of the political establishment to murky public conveniences ... it constantly proves touching and entertaining, with a sharp period flavour ... There are moments ... that come close to the emotional depth of Rattigan at his finest, others that equal the gamey period flavour of the undervalued Rodney Ackland." Charles Spencer, *Daily Telegraph*

"Britain has changed, if a little bit too late for the Gielgud generation. All credit to de Jongh for telling us this in so lively, arresting a play." Benedict Nightingale, *The Times*

"Entertainingly old-fashioned, poignant and often very funny ... It would be unfair if *Plague Over England* were to be pigeon-holed as a gay play. It's really a richly characterized study of human foibles around gay themes ... it's cheerfully combative, kind-hearted and optimistic, with these "artistic gentlemen" using all their wit and courage to triumph over the grey, dour forces of conformity." Charles Hart, *Sunday Times*

"*Plague Over England* is funny, angry, moving, refreshing and fantastically entertaining. One looks forward to the next work from this highly original pen." Lloyd Evans, *Spectator*

"In his terrific first play he sensitively traces a lost world." Johann Hari, *Evening Standard*

Plague Over England

A play

Nicholas de Jongh

Samuel French — London
www.samuelfrench-london.co.uk

PLAGUE OVER ENGLAND

First produced by Chantelle Staynings and Neil McPherson at the Finborough Theatre on 29th February 2008 with the following cast:

Detective Chief Inspector Bellinger	Steve Hansell
Rayner, Lord Goddard/	
Dr Ambrose Quentin	David Barnaby
Mr Justice Percival Lightbourne/	
Binkie Beaumont	Simon Dutton
Peter Munroe	Steve Hansell
Police Constable Terry Fordham	Leon Ockenden
Matthew Barnsbury	Timothy Watson
Dame Sybil Thorndike/	
Vera Dromgoole	Nichola McAuliffe
Sir John Gielgud	Jasper Britton
Gregory Lightbourne	Robin Whiting
Chiltern Moncreiffe/	
Sir David Maxwell Fyfe	John Warnaby
Brian Mandeville/Bert/Fred/	
Douglas Witherby	David Burt

Directed by Tamara Harvey
Designed by Alex Marker
Lighting by James Farncombe
Sound design by Colin Pink
Costume design by Penn O'Gara

Produced by Bill Kenwright and the Ambassador Theatre Group at the Duchess Theatre, London on 19th February 2009 with the following changes in cast:

Rayner, Lord Goddard/	
Dr Ambrose Quentin	Hugh Ross
Gregory Lightbourne	Sam Heughan
Matthew Barnsbury	Michael Brown
Dame Sybil Thorndike/Vera Dromgoole	Celia Imrie
Sir John Gielgud	Michael Feast

Sound design by Theo Holloway
Costume design by Trish Wilkinson
Original music by Alexander S. Bermange with lyrics by Nicholas de Jongh

COPYRIGHT INFORMATION

(See also page iv)

CONTENTS

CHARACTERS

The name of Peter Munroe from the Finborough and West End productions has been changed to Daniel Arlington in this Acting Edition.

Detective Chief Inspector Bellinger, about 36
Rayner, **Lord Goddard**, Lord Chief Justice of
    England and Wales
Mr Justice Percival Lightbourne, a High Court
    Judge
Daniel Arlington, 40ish, American
Police Constable Terry Fordham, early/mid twenties
Matthew Barnsbury, civil servant
Dame Sybil Thorndike, actress
Sir John Gielgud, 49, later 71
Dr Ambrose Quentin
Gregory Lightbourne, 19, later 41
Douglas Witherby, manager, Dudmaston Mews
    public lavatory; waiter at the Polynaeum
Vera Dromgoole, retired actress, owner of Queen Mab's
Brian Mandeville, Vera's partner at Queen Mab's
Chiltern Moncreiffe, theatre critic
Sir David Maxwell Fyfe, Home Secretary
Bert, news vendor
Binkie Beaumont, Managing Director of H.M.
    Tennent, the dominant play-producing company
    during the 1950s
Fred, doorman

The characters of Douglas, Bert and Fred should all be played by the same actor.

PRODUCTION NOTES

The basic setting is of a Victorian lavatory and its framework remains in view throughout. There should be no attempt at detailed realism or laborious changes of setting. This is not quite a realistic play and it's essential that scenes flow into each other, with the dissolves between scenes rendered with music and characters from the end of one scene either remaining *in situ* until those for the next arrive. The lavatory's back or side walls can revolve to disclose Queen Mab's cocktail cabinet, the Home Secretary's office, the Polynaeum and other locations. Back projections must be used for the external scenes, such as St James's Park, Hyde Park and the Haymarket. This should help to give a strong, atmospheric or period sense of London. Such a device may be used for other scenes too.

In Act II, Scene 5, asterixes between dialogue indicate the shifts in focus between the two scenes taking place simultaneously on opposite sides of the stage. It is left to the individual director to decide how he or she wishes to make this distinction.

Where voices, singing and shouting are heard off stage (for example from the Piano Bar at Queen Mab's or during the gay activists' demonstration in the final scene) these may be spoken by actors who are not on stage or by stage management, unless otherwise indicated in the effects plot.

The music for the songs "I'm Pretty" in Act I, Scene 8, "Hi There..." in Act I, Scene 8, "I'm Katie the Cook" in Act I, Scene 8", "Miss Jessica Tandy" in Act I, Scene 10 and "Seeker" in Act II, Scenes 3 and 13 was written by Alexander S. Bermange, lyrics by Nicholas de Jongh. It is available on hire from Samuel French Ltd and there will be an additional performance fee for it use (see page iv). Alexander S. Bermange also has optional backing tracks and incidental music for the play which would be the subject of a separate arrangement between Mr Bermange and producing companies. Contact details are available from the Editorial Department at Samuel French.

ACKNOWLEDGEMENTS

The productions of *Plague Over England* at the Finborough Theatre in 2008 and Duchess Theatre in 2009 came about as the result of the help and practical assistance of a large number of people, apart, of course, from those directly involved in bringing the play to the stage.

The author would like to express his gratitude to:

Keith Baxter, Sam Beazley, Colin Bell, Susan Black, Todd Boyce, Jack Bradley, Nica Burns, Matthew Byam Shaw, Ned Chaillet, Julian Cole, Jeremy Connor, Dominic Cooke, Kathy Dacre, Don Davidson, Gary Davy, Jean Diamond, David Eldridge, Sonia Friedman, Michael Grandage, Thelma Holt, Lucy Hume, Lord Hutchinson, Angela Hyde Courtney, Sue Hyman, Cliff Johannou, Jeremy Kingston, Peter Lantos, Andrew Lumsden, Sean Mathias, Simon McDermott, Wendy Moffat, Daniel Novelli, Howard Panter, Paul Rhys, Ian Rickson, James Roose-Evans, David Roper, Lady Rothermere, Brian Sewell, Timothy Sheader, Amanda Smith, Rosemary Squire, Matthew Todd, *Whatsonstage*, and all those who were involved in two rehearsed readings, first in the bar of the Duchess Theatre and then on the main stage of the Royal Court.

For Bill Kenwright and Neil McPherson
and in loving memory of
Adrian Ffooks (1955 - 1996)
— beautiful, brave and beset by
homophobia.

ACT I

The framework of a Victorian lavatory remains in view throughout the play. It should resemble a relic. There are flickers of lamplight from outside — an orange glow and impression of 1950s evening mist/smog. This antique urinal is full of faint lavatorial murmurs, drips and gushes of water. The urinals, where you piss on to china and whose pipes are polished to a leering, come-hitherish gleam, stand R in two rows. The Victorian wash basins are equipped with ancient taps. There is a small cubicle with frosted-glass windows by the entrance, from which Witherby will appear and into which he retreats

Scene 1

Hyde Park. 1953, twilight

A back projection shows a timeless view of Hyde Park — as it is now, so it was in 1953, though bushes, trees and shrubs loomed smaller. A second film projection gives a distant aspect of a cruising area in the park. We can see shadowy figures, some standing under trees, one or two moving

Two men, Lord Goddard and Chief Inspector Bellinger, stand in the reflected glow of Bellinger's torchlight that faintly illuminates them. Goddard has an opulent pair of binoculars hanging from his neck. In the distance can be seen a dozen tiny illuminations — lit cigarettes — which flicker around

Bellinger You know how they attract each other's attention in the dark, my Lord?

Goddard (*humorously*) I shudder to think.

Bellinger They flash a cigarette, sir. Sometimes they ask to be lit up.

Goddard (*jovially*) It sounds almost civilized. (*He raises the binoculars to his eyes*) I suppose I ought to take a look.

Bellinger I wouldn't recommend it, sir. You won't like it.

Goddard Like it? I'm not here for pleasure, Bellinger. The still, small voice of duty. It drives me on.

Bellinger Naturally, sir.

Goddard (*letting the binoculars fall*) Bellinger. Do my eyes deceive me? Two of them. Kissing. Does it happen often? (*He hands the binoculars to Bellinger*)

Bellinger takes a cursory look and returns the binoculars to Goddard

Bellinger We do come across it, my Lord. But it's not a usual practice at all.

A cigarette light flares

Goddard Thank God for that. To think the friendly Woodbine can be so misused! Imagine an innocent, courting couple! Stumbling on a scene like this.

Bellinger No danger, sir. These days normal folk give Hyde Park a wide berth once twilight falls.

Goddard I didn't realize the place was infested.

Bellinger We'll clear them out in the end, my Lord. We've got the park under regular watch.

A sound of human, not police whistles, then the cigarette lights are extinguished. Torch lights gleam

Goddard Bellinger! That whistling?

Bellinger Yes, my Lord. Our boys. Operation Everest. (*He looks at his watch*) Dead on time. We're hoping for quite a big catch tonight.

Goddard That's the spirit!

An owl hoots

Such an ominous warble! The owl's!

Bellinger I think you'll find it's one of our men, my Lord, imitating nature. They develop a flair for sniffing out your lurkers.

Police whistles. Big lights begin to circle. A magnified voice: "Stop. Police. Don't move."

Goddard Such reassuring words!

Bellinger We're raiding St James's Park tonight as well, my Lord. Always a few guardsmen peddling their wares.

Goddard It beggars belief. In my young day guardsmen wouldn't have dreamed of putting their vital body parts out to rent.

Shouts and cries. More police whistles. A concentration of lights and suddenly a howl of fear

Bellinger gazes raptly. Goddard's eyes are not up to it. He pants with excitement

Bellinger? What's happening? Have they caught someone in the act? (*Breathing heavily*) Yes? Well? Yes? Bellinger!
Bellinger (*chuckling*) I'll be blowed. Cheeky bugger! One of them's making a run for it. Tearing away like a stag. Three of ours giving chase. Yes, yes. Come on, lads. Yes — gotcha!
Goddard (*thrilled, an exultant gasp of excitement emanating from him*) Aah!
Bellinger They've brought him down my Lord. Terrific tackle. Look at him struggle. Like a wild cat.
Goddard (*still breathing unevenly*) Yes — I've seen enough, Bellinger. Yes. It's high time I left the playing fields of Sodom and Gomorrah.
Bellinger Of course, my Lord. It's no place for a gentleman.
Goddard I feel a little faint. There's brandy in the Bentley for succour and my manservant's made us roast beef sandwiches ... Do join me. (*He moves away*)
Bellinger Very kind, my Lord ...

Shouts of "Make a run for it." Police whistles again

Goddard (*as they begin to leave*) How many did you net last year, Bellinger?
Bellinger More than a hundred sir. Here in Hyde Park.
Goddard Terrifying — such numbers!
Bellinger It's the youngsters I worry about, my Lord. I've a couple of teenage lads myself. I want them to grow up proper, in a better class of England.
Goddard Admirable! We'll drink a toast to the new Queen and England — reborn — where men are men!

They walk out, Bellinger helping Goddard

SCENE 2

The High Court

Music — "Zadok the Priest" by Handel plays, then fades out

Mr Justice Percival Lightbourne walks through the urinal to the front of stage to deliver his speech to the audience. He is a grand, bewigged figure, dressed in the scarlet robing of the High Court. He speaks in the judicial mode, quietly without a shred of emotion or rhetoric — he must not sound theatrical

Lightbourne I simply do not understand what is happening to this great nation of ours. An epidemic of male vice is spreading through the land. Each year more and more young men are brought to the courts, having been irrevocably seduced into indecent practices by their elders, fated never to achieve normal, happy married life or father children.

Tunbridge Wells is just the latest city to succumb to this epidemic. The jury by its findings has corroborated the prosecution's case that a single invert can coax scores of young men into the homosexual life. The judiciary's supreme duty is to protect the moral values of our realm. Those values are now gravely beset by stress and strain. Crimes of violence, juvenile delinquency and sexual laxity increase annually ... It seems as if we are running adrift on a rising tide of fornication and drunkenness. Even our cultural glory is besmirched by novels and drama that regard adultery as a joke and homosexuality as a fit subject for discussion.

Charles Applethwaite, as Managing Director of a leading toiletry company, lay magistrate and Chairman of Tunbridge Wells Conservative Association, you were regarded as a pillar of the community. Today that pillar falls. You have been found guilty of grave and unnatural offences. A soldier, electrician, dustman, plumber, fireman, chauffeur and pest control officer all succumbed to your advances. On the pretext of offering these young men the chance to view your newly acquired television set — one of the few in Tunbridge Wells — you organized a school of instruction in homosexual vice.

Sadly there are no available facilities that would afford you the medical and psychiatric treatment which might lead to a cure. You will go to prison for three years.

The music of "Zadok the Priest" returns, then fades

SCENE 3

The Serpentine. Night

A back projection of the shimmering, moonlit expanse of the Serpentine, on which lamplight plays as well. On the other side of the waters can be dimly glimpsed an evening landscape of trees against a moody sky-line

There are two park benches

A man, Daniel, fortyish, a bit the better for alcohol, sits on one of the benches. He has a silver flask from which he sometimes drinks. It is getting dark. We hear the distant cries and whistles of the police raid of the first scene

A handsome, muscular young man in his early twenties, Terry Fordham, stands by the waterfront, his body not quite facing it. He smokes, is placed to be able to see the other night visitor and glances back at him a couple of times

Daniel Nice night.
Terry (*not looking round*) Yeah.
Daniel Sounds like trouble over there.
Terry Want to watch yourself here, mate. Hunting queers, that's what they do at night.
Daniel Yeah. Same where I come from.
Terry (*turning round*) Yeah? Nothing against them myself. The poofs. But —
Daniel Some of them are OK guys.
Terry Could be. (*He moves over towards Daniel and the bench*) You a Yank then?
Daniel Sure. (*He drinks from the flask, offers it to Terry*)

Terry shakes his head

Daniel You live around here?
Terry In Kensington? Must be joking!
Daniel I'm down Holland Park way. Cigarette?
Terry Nah, mate, I'm in training, aren't I. (*He looks at his watch*) Gotta get going. Sorry.
Daniel See you again?
Terry Yeah. Why not ...?

Daniel stands up. They shake hands

Terry leaves

Daniel walks down to the water, stands there listening, turns and comes back to the bench, sits down

Another young man, Matthew, dressed in corduroy trousers, suede shoes and a dark jacket comes walking quite slowly along the walk-way by the water. He shimmers with nerves. He cruises Daniel, darting a quick look at him as he passes. He walks on a little and then turns round to look back for a moment, then sits down at the other bench. He casts another furtive glance at Daniel

Daniel watches this exercise

Daniel Hey, man! Could I trouble you to light me up?
Matthew (*flustered*) Sorry? I didn't quite hear that …
Daniel Matches?
Matthew I'm so sorry. I don't smoke.
Daniel (*finding matches in a back pocket*) Ah, one more box! How you doing, Buddy.
Matthew You're American! What a relief!
Daniel Yeah. I give relief. And get it. (*He lights a cigarette*)
Matthew (*uncomprehending but enthralled*) You see — I thought you might be one of them ——
Daniel One of which?
Matthew Agent provocateur. Queer basher.
Daniel No. I try to be friendly to queers.
Matthew How fascinating! One meets so few Americans. Except round Piccadilly Circus.
Daniel Why don't you come over?
Matthew (*looking around*) Would it be safe?
Daniel You could sit eighteen inches away — if you're worried. Or even two feet.
Matthew Suppose a police car drives up?
Daniel They don't come down here ... Anyway we could always pretend to be friends.
Matthew Oh, really? (*He goes to Daniel; hesitant*) I'm mad about Americans. Marlon Brando — *Streetcar Named Desire*. (*He stands poised*) James Dean — you know.
Daniel Yeah — I get your taste. Hey! Be daring. Sit down.
Matthew Well I do rather want to.

Daniel You're OK with me. (*He puts out a hand*) Dan.
Matthew (*shaking his hand*) Matthew. I really shouldn't be doing this.
Daniel Why? You haven't done anything ——
Matthew Well not exactly. (*He sits down*)
Daniel That's swell. (*He offers the flask to Matthew*)

Matthew shakes his head

Matthew What d'you do?
Daniel I guess you could find out ——
Matthew You an actor? You over here in a musical?
Daniel (*amused*) Hell no! I seem theatrical?
Matthew On no — no. You look — awfully athletic.
Daniel What about you?
Matthew Oh I'm not very interesting at all.
Daniel You want to come back?
Matthew Are you near?
Daniel Kensington.
Matthew That sounds respectable. You live alone?
Daniel Sure. Be my guest.
Matthew Oh yes please. It's hard to resist. (*He looks at Daniel; flirtatious*) And I won't. I'd be mad to refuse.
Daniel (*standing up*) Sure you'd be mad. Come. You can be crazy with me.

SCENE 4

The Haymarket theatre

John Gielgud and Sybil Thorndike are rehearsing "A Day by the Sea". They sometimes refer to scripts. Sybil stands at a tiny table and arranges flowers in a vase. She speaks to a present but unseen character. She is a bit nervous. Quotation marks are used where Gielgud and Sybil speak as characters in their play — the elderly middle-class mother, Laura, and her unmarried, diplomat son

Sybil "Of course he's absurdly single-minded. (*Calling out*) Julian! If only I could have persuaded him to marry, I'm sure it would have given him more balance. Some cheerful, young person. It would have made him ... (*Calling more loudly*) Julian! (*Calling*) Julian, do come out."

Pause

Gielgud "I'd forgotten we had all those azaleas." (*He shakes his head*) Sorry, Sybil. I'll try that again. I sounded so affected. "I'd forgotten we had all those azaleas. When was I last here in May?"

Sybil (*with too much vehemence*) "You may well ask. (*Speaking to another unseen character*) He's never at home now. Never! He's always organizing Europe."

Gielgud Wonderful, darling, but perhaps a little less hectic. It's so difficult. I'm putting you off with all this azalea nonsense ... Would my character even notice such suburban flowers? Let's chop it out. I should come on all aquiver with tension and nerves.

Sybil John, dear, we open in Liverpool next week. It's too late for chopping and changing. We've done as much as we can to beef up the scene ...

Gielgud Of course — they're such conventional characters. They never surprise you.

Sybil Well, they're all sort of English Chekhovian — pining for old times.

Gielgud This country-house melancholia and post-war gloom in the lower depths of Lyme Regis. Who wants it?

Sybil Melancholia goes down very well in the stalls these days, dear. Audiences like a little down-lift. They want to see the middle-classes making do in grand Dorset houses ...

Gielgud It seems to get more old-hat the longer we rehearse.

Sybil Not at all, dear. It's quite faithful. Middle-aged England after the war and under the weather. Anglo-Saxons secretly turbulent ...

Gielgud I like a little turbulence. Should we carry on, darling?

Sybil We certainly should ——

Gielgud (*nodding*) That difficult bit.

Sybil and Gielgud turn the pages of their scripts

"Yes, I'm afraid I've been a disappointment to you."

Sybil (*vehemently*) "It's for you that I mind, dear. I don't like to think of you going into middle age unsuccessful and alone — it's such a bleak outlook. Independence is all very well for a young man, but as you grow older you'll find it's just another name for loneliness."

Gielgud "Mother!"

Sybil "I'm talking, Julian."

Gielgud "I'm sorry but could we discuss that later, do you mind?"

Sybil "Yes. I do mind. I'm speaking for your own good and I'll be grateful if you allow me to finish."

Gielgud "I beg your pardon." No, no that's far too lower-middle class. Surely I wouldn't sound so servile?

Sybil I don't know, dear. I haven't had servants for years.

Gielgud Of course you haven't. Nor I really. Should I try standing? All tense. No. Sitting and shocked by your words? That's it. Bowed down. Yes? Or very upright in the deckchair. Trying to be poised. No! No! All too artificial. I can't make my character real.

Sybil Johnnie! You've got it all. Don't worry.

Gielgud (*pleased*) Really? Well, thank you. I suppose I shouldn't try so hard to be natural. Now when you're warning me about loneliness – what about trying it cooler, more *piano*?

Sybil Darling, if we don't get dramatic here, if we don't bring it up now, when will we? I mean we're in Act Three. We've come to the crisis — I'm afraid you won't ever get hitched — I'm wondering whether you're — well — not the marrying sort.

Gielgud That's a bit near the knuckle, isn't it?

Sybil The Foreign Office won't promote you until you've a nice wife to show off ...

Gielgud I've put all my drive into work.

Sybil John — the audience will understand. Even if they pretend they can't.

Gielgud But I've just asked Frances to marry me.

Sybil Yes, dear. She tried to get you twenty years ago. You've never even noticed her before. You only want to marry to save your career. You're a confirmed bachelor. Surely they're side-lined in the Diplomatic world ...

Gielgud (*disturbed*) Well I couldn't possibly make it that obvious ——

Sybil Of course, darling. I'd just be yourself if I were you! That'll be quite enough!

Gielgud (*thoughtful*) Yes. Sybil dear, take it from "Why don't you let me help you?"

Sybil "But now you're going to be home for a time I could easily do some entertaining for you. I should enjoy it. And you could meet a few nice people. For instance how long is it since you've seen the Comptons? Elizabeth is twenty-six now and she's grown into such a nice creature."

Gielgud "Yes, I dare say — but." (*He captures Julian's desolation from here on*)

Sybil "Very well. Then I shall arrange it."

Gielgud "Mother, will you please try to understand that I'm not interested in Elizabeth Clinton. I'm sure she's extremely attractive as you say, but the fact is that I bore her and she bores me."

Sybil "What nonsense!"

Gielgud "I don't know why it is, but I make her nervous. Then either she can't talk to me at all or else she can't stop." Now — here you can take it up a bit more, Sybil.

Sybil "I can see what it is — you'll never marry, dear."

Gielgud "Mother!"

Sybil (*on the verge of tears*) "You'll simply end up one of those pathetic creatures who spend their days in clubs for company and go home night after night to empty flats. Very well. I shall say no more. But if you imagine that's a happy way to live." Golly. It does hot up nicely doesn't it?

Gielgud Very poignant. You let everything out in the open. Or as out as you dare.

Sybil He's not very self-aware is he?

Gielgud Remaining a bit of a mystery to oneself. Much the best way.

Sybil That's what I like. Audiences come to see characters taking trips to the heart of darkness.

Gielgud You make it sound like missionary work in Africa ...

Sybil It's not that different in deepest Dorset. And you're making it beautifully sad.

Gielgud Just my bundle of tricks. I wish I dared join the avant garde. That extraordinary new John Whiting play ... I didn't quite have the guts.

Sybil Take risks, Johnnie. A little daring — no bad thing.

Gielgud Really?

Sybil I wish I still had the chance: nowadays I'm just offered respectable old ladies arranging flowers and other people's lives in Lyme Regis.

Gielgud That's it. The prison of drawing-room dramatics.

Sybil (*ironic*) If only we could break out — have the chance to be different ——

Gielgud (*lightly*) Oh no! Not at our age, darling. Just think! It might cause a serious scandal.

SCENE 5

Doctor Ambrose Quentin's office

A desk and two chairs. The elderly doctor and Matthew Barnsbury

Matthew It's like an addiction. I can't control it. I've got to fall in love in the normal way, get married, have children.

Doctor (*scribbling*) Quite right! Very proper! We're going to get you to snap out of it. Now one crucial thing — what's your line of business?

Matthew Oh, I'm afraid it's confidential.

Doctor Nothing you say goes further than my medical records.

Matthew No, no! I daren't.

Doctor (*displeased*) This isn't a pleasant business, Mr Barnsbury. You're making my task much harder.

Matthew (*pained*) No. No. (*Pause*) Where I work, if they discover you're a — it's ruin. If you're not married by thirty, if you've not got a girl the gossip starts ——

Doctor Quite so. Ghastly predicament. I've had chaps in your position before. Look — I'm going to be frank with you, Mr Barnsbury.

Matthew Thanks.

Doctor You see you're a public school chap — you're not to blame. You follow me?

Matthew Not exactly.

Doctor Public schools! Breeding ground for no end of queer malarkey, I'm afraid ... Adolescence — risky time! All those hormones and urges leaping around in your body ... Temptations all over the place. You fall for that muscular hooker in the first fifteen. Or it could be that pretty fag with nice, blond curls. I remember it well. One thing leads to a bit of the other. You go too far in the dormitory. Oh yes! Shame and guilt! Now your normal fellow. He grows out of it. But your queer chap — he's stuck. Like a car jammed in reverse. That's where I come in — to give you a good kick-start.

Matthew It sounds alarming.

Doctor Not at all. Our Electric Aversion therapy — by golly, it works. It's the coming thing.

Matthew I've heard it gives you violent headaches.

Doctor Well, sometimes! But what's the odd headache, if you end up cured, Mr Barnsbury? It works wonders for sex offenders in prison — and your sort. Now, take your oestrogen.

Matthew I'm not touching it!

Doctor That's the spirit. It's dangerous. I wouldn't want you landing up with lady breasts and your member stranded for life in the resting position. Electricity's the thing ... Have you put right and gallivanting with girls in three shakes of a lamb's tail. (*He stands up and draws down a screen which shows a film montage of young men dressed in nothing but swimming trunks*) Now take a look at these likely lads. Any take your fancy?

Matthew (*gazing*) Well, yes ...

Doctor Don't be shy. A few? Several? Lots?

Matthew (*gazing*) Most — just three or four leave me cold.

Doctor Very good. You're doing frightfully well. Now I'm afraid this may embarrass you a bit.

A new film montage shows, of the same men, naked

Here they are — same fellows. A bit of an eyeful, I'm afraid. In their
birthday suits. How d'you feel about them?

Matthew (*duly embarrassed*) Enthusiastic, I'm afraid …

Doctor Don't be shy — you've got a bit stirred up in the lower regions,
haven't you?

Matthew Yes — more or less ——

Doctor Oh, excellent! Well done! Now I'm going to introduce you to
a couple of chaps — Percy Major and Percy Minor. (*He rummages
in drawer and produces two black boxes to which electrodes are
attached; he holds them up*) Here you are! What d'you think?

Matthew (*bemused*) I don't know.

Doctor Well you and the Percies are going to get seriously attached to
each other in the next few weeks.

Matthew And this is electric aversion treatment?

Doctor They're my electricity miracle workers. Attach one to your leg.
And I start giving you shocks — nothing to worry about. Just a bit of
discomfort.

Matthew How does it work though?

Doctor It's our behavioural method, Mr Barnsbury. You get to associate
attractive chaps with nasty shocks. Soon starts to turn you off homo
thoughts. You feel stirrings in your lower regions. Then an electric tap
— like a slap on the buttocks …

Matthew I see.

The Doctor straps electrodes to Matthew's leg

Doctor Now just you relax, Mr Barnsbury. Nothing to worry about. Just
a bit of a prick as they say in the services.

Matthew But the shocks?

Doctor It's all so gradual you'll hardly notice. I go gently at first.

Matthew Thank God!

Doctor And then you'll be practising yourself with Percy at home. The
pictures come one at a time. (*He begins to press a buzzer on his desk*)
Ready to have a go?

Matthew Yes.

Doctor Jolly good.

A series of projections of naked young men starts

Matthew Yes that's all right. I can feel it a bit.

Doctor Getting excited?

Matthew I'm too afraid for that.

Doctor Just relax. Enjoy yourself!

More projections, quicker

Matthew Yes! Yes! Oh, that hurts — that hurts! Oh, God! (*He gets up and tears off the electrodes*)

The projections stop

No, Dr Letts, no! This is all madness.

Matthew walks out

Doctor (*to himself, shaking his head*) I don't know. One gives them the chance of a helping hand and they haven't got the courage to grasp it. That's queers for you, I'm afraid.

Doctor walks out

Scene 6

The Dudmaston Mews public lavatory

The interior is deserted. Douglas Witherby, the lavatory attendant, in overalls and plastic gloves, a pail with scrubbing brush, Gumption, Ibcol, Duraglit, shoe-cleaning brushes, cleaning cloths and mop by his side stands close to the manager's cubicle. He is a sweet, garrulous and rather effeminate man, beset by loneliness. It's important not to make him threatening or weird

Greg, a young man, about nineteen, broad, sturdy and muscular strolls in with assumed casualness. He wears an open-necked white shirt, dark blazers and oatmeal trousers. Witherby observes him go to the urinal stall, taking in the view as he goes. Witherby pauses from his polishing, watches him, perhaps realizing his newcomer status

Witherby Evening, sir.
Greg (*embarrassed*) Evening. (*He turns around after urinating*)

Witherby waits for him

Witherby How's the world treating you, sir?
Greg Well I can't complain.
Witherby So you've taken a shine to my convenience?
Greg (*startled*) Oh no, I happened to be passing and I needed ——

Witherby You've got good taste, I can tell. Go on, don't be shy. Have
a stare. They don't make them like this any more. Oh no. It may only
be a council WC. but it's got real, Victorian class.

Greg (*forced into awareness, dutifully looking up and down*) I'm not
very familiar with lavatories.

Witherby Just look at those mosaic floors. The lovely green tiles. The
mahogany doors. And those marble barriers between urinals?

Greg What's the point of them?

Witherby Those Victorians took a firm line with below the waist
matters. No friskiness allowed. Stopped you peeking at the next door
chap's personals.

Greg Of course.

Witherby Tell you what, sir — if you don't mind my mentioning ——

Greg What?

Witherby Your shoes, sir.

Greg looks down

Lost their dazzle. Could do with a firm brush and polish. I give a free
service.

Greg (*bemused*) For what?

Witherby (*approaching*) Just you let my brushes loose on you, sir, and
we'll soon have them all perky again. I'm known for my technique.

Greg (*bemused*) All right.

Witherby proceeds to kneel, brush and polish, to Greg's embarrassment

Very pretty indeed.

Witherby Yes. These urinals are your genuine Spode. The old Queen
Mary — she'd just the same. For her tea service. I was pals with her
page boy — the things he knew about the Duke of Windsor. The
trouble he had with his private parts! But hush my mouth.

Greg (*interested at last*) Really! What was wrong?

Witherby Oh he was always premature until he met the duchess. But
I mustn't gossip. I feel for the new queen. My loose tongue. Slap!
Slap! (*Quickly changing subject*) I care about hygiene, I do ... I use
Gumption, Chemico and Duraglit. You won't see stains in here. You
see artistes drop in. They have to have cleanliness.

Greg (*intrigued*) Anyone famous?

Witherby (*with pride*) Stars of stage and screen and the Houses of
Parliament. I mustn't name names.

Greg (*deadpan*) But no impropriety?

Witherby Nothing like that, sir. We've respectable married gents too.
They like things proper. I won't have riff-raff loitering.

Greg How d'you deal with them?
Witherby "Get on with it," I say. "And don't make a meal of it." It's hard these days. Spivs and Teddy boys in winklepickers, flashing flick-knives, fiddling with their bits and pieces. I ask you!
Greg You're talking about daytime?
Witherby Oh we never close. Just like Raymond's Revue Bar.
Greg But you can't be here all the time?
Witherby No — I've my night job you see. It's untended after seven. I'm afraid ... That's when things sometimes get frisky ... There you are! Come up a treat!
Greg Amazing. Thanks.
Witherby If you don't mind my saying sir. (*Pause*) Keep an eye cocked down here. The pretty police drop by — you only have to smile or nod your member in the wrong direction and you're done for.
Greg (*leaving*) Thanks. Thanks. (*He hands Witherby a sixpence*)
Witherby Well I'm obliged, sir. (*As Greg goes*) See you down here again, I hope, but watch out!

Witherby returns to his cubicle humming "I'll see you again"

Greg goes out

SCENE 7

There are two chairs on stage

Terry makes a striking impression as he stands ill at ease. His prettiness is qualified by his size and muscularity. He moves with an athlete's limber ease. He exudes a sexual ambiguity that makes him a natural candidate for the pretty policeman's role. He sits in one of the chairs

Chief Inspector Stephen Bellinger walks in with a large bag. Terry stands up. Bellinger's manner is both ingratiating and confident. Handsome in the sleek, clean-cut way required of the pretty policeman he was many years ago. He deposits the bag on the floor with care

Bellinger (*holding out a hand*) Welcome to the Vice, Public Lavatories, C Division, Constable. You'll be doing Chelsea, you lucky boy!
Terry (*shaking Bellinger's hand*) Yes, sir. Thank you, sir.
Bellinger Got your first night coming up, Terry. Chance to shine.
Terry I'm very worried, sir.
Bellinger I know — you new boys — afraid your pride and joy's going to get into the wrong hands.

Terry Well, sir, they told me I gotta join the squad. I really don't want to. It's not right for me.

Bellinger Look Terry, you've been chosen. It's an honour. Government wants us to get a fresh grip on male vice.

Terry (*doubtfully*) I don't like trapping queers. Poor bastards. It's not fair.

Bellinger Law's the law, Terry. Some lads — they'd give their right arm to be in the Vice.

Terry I'd sooner have it for my own use, sir. I wouldn't know what to do without it.

Bellinger Very good, Terry. I'm all for a copper who likes a laugh. You married then?

Terry Can't say I am, sir.

Bellinger Walking out with a girl regular?

Terry (*embarrassed*) Not quite.

Bellinger Never mind. You're a good looking lad. I can tell you're one for the ladies.

Terry Well they do come on to me — Friday nights ...

Bellinger And very nice too. Now. Let's start with your proselytizer.

Terry gets out a notebook and begins to write throughout Bellinger's lesson

Know what a proselytizer is, lad?

Terry (*bemused*) It's not something do with a fertiliser, is it?

Bellinger (*shakes head*) Good shot, Terry. You could say he spreads it around — your proselytizer. He's your average queer. And he's always up to recruit new members.

Terry To what?

Bellinger I call it a tribe myself. The secret homo world ... Now, males persistently importuning males for immoral purposes. What's that mean to you?

Terry Queers looking for queers.

Bellinger Ah, it's a tricky one! You see your homo — he gets bored of doing it with his own sort. He fancies bending a hetero.

Terry You don't have to tell me, sir. I've had advances.

Bellinger Yes, a copper never knows what's coming up behind him. (*He permits himself a grim smile*) That's enough of the sir, lad. It's Steve and Terry now.

Terry Thanks, Steve.

Bellinger Well, tonight Terry, you'll be in queer dress. And we'll rehearse you for importuning.

Terry But I'm not dressed up like one of them.

Bellinger Don't you worry. Your clobber's supplied. (*He produces a pair of tight jeans and a tee shirt from the carrier bag*) Right little agent provocateur, you'll look.

Terry I dunno, Steve. It's all Greek to me.

Bellinger It's French, Terry. Means you've got what it takes!

Terry Well, I never!

Bellinger These new American jeans. (*He fondly displays them*) Flown over special. Tight as your British drainpipe. Shows your private parts off a treat. (*He puts them down*)

Terry I dunno, Steve. I don't want them having a stare at my ... (*He stops*)

Bellinger (*sympathizing*) I'll be outside in the car. Takes time to get into it, the pretty police business.

Terry I'll be all alone in there?

Bellinger You'll soon have company. (*He smiles*) Now your queers, you see, Terry, they're different ——

Terry From what?

Bellinger They're not like us. Sex — it's their one serious interest. And fancy clothes and musicals of course. They've their special pubs and clubs. Own secret language too ...

Terry I didn't know they spoke different.

Bellinger Polari. Strange lingo.

Terry Will I have to learn it?

Bellinger (*with grim relish*) No, lad. You'll only speak the Queen's English with them. Now cruising? Know about that?

Terry Is it a queer walk?

Bellinger Clever boy! Yes, it's when they're on the hunt for open-air sex ... They move so slow — till they see their prey.

Terry Sounds a bit nasty.

Bellinger Sad thing is they can't find love — the poor bastards.

Terry Why's that then, Steve?

Bellinger They're stuffed with all the wrong hormones ... That's why they're never satisfied of course ...

Terry Can't they love their own way?

Bellinger (*shaking his head*) Thing is, Terry. They can't be satisfied with just one man.

Terry Is that why they're always after sex?

Bellinger (*delighted*) There you are! You've got the picture! Now, you ever done acting before, Terry? School? Youth club?

Terry Nah. I did woodwork and football, didn't I?

Bellinger I'm going to turn you into a proper little Laurence Olivier. Right. I'll play queer. You'll be pretty police.

Terry I'll never get used to doing this.

Bellinger First night nerves, Terry. We'll have a nice pint when we come off duty.

Terry I'll need something stiffer.

Bellinger Oh you're a joker, Terry. You'll be a new man after your first arrest.

Terry I'm happy with the man I am, Steve.

Bellinger Come on! Stand at the pisser. You've got your equipment out.

Terry (*embarrassed*) Now?

Bellinger No, lad, no. This is your dress rehearsal. The undress comes later. You mime.

Terry Mime?

Bellinger You pretend; you put on a show.

Terry What for?

Bellinger Stone the poodles! To show interest. Undo your buttons.

Terry reluctantly mimes

Play hard to get. Play cocky.

Terry overdoes it

Stop poncing around. Act natural. Now watch me. (*He parodies a gay man cruising for sex*)

Terry You're a natural, Steve.

Bellinger Now, Terry, tempt me. Come on to me. I'm a vicar, unhappily married with two kids and unnatural tendencies, up from Tunbridge Wells to meet some top bishops to talk about keeping in touch with God. I've drunk three glasses of sherry in a posh gentlemen's club up West. I've got myself randy. I shoot you a glance. And what do you do?

Terry Give you a reassuring wink?

Bellinger He's under your spell, lad. What he wants is for you to toss him off, or vice versa.

Terry I don't want to get my hands dirty, Steve. I really don't.

Bellinger You never get down to it. Just one flash of their offending member or even an approving smile ... You've got 'im. So I turn my gentleman's cock to you. And what you look for then?

Terry See if he's all excited.

Bellinger (*nodding*) And see if he's cut or uncut. His offending member — it may be used in evidence.

Terry I dunno ——

Bellinger So the trap closes. (*He moves over, mimes the action*) He winks. He smiles. He stares. He's done for. He comes over. He's done for. He looks and tries to touch it. He's nicked. You grab him. You flash your warrant card.

Terry Do I do up my buttons first?

Bellinger Don't worry about buttons, lad! You say "I'm a police officer. I'm arresting you for persistently importuning male persons for immoral purposes. Anything you say may be taken down and used in evidence against you." That's the ticket!

Bellinger walks out

Terry (*alone*) Christ, how do I get myself out of this? (*He changes his voice*) I'm an agent provocateur doing my duty for queen and country. You're under arrest. I can't help it if you're married. You shouldn't have tried to touch it. What's that you're offering me? Fifty pounds? You're trying to corrupt me with cash? Don't you know a British policeman never ever takes a bribe? Unless it's a big one.

SCENE 8

Queen Mab's. Early evening

Queen Mab's is a Soho private members' club founded during the Second World War and intended as a refuge for the gay bohemian and cultural coteries that flowered from the 1930s and are now withering. The place basks in déjà vu, is redolent of temps perdu. It is furnished with elderly theatre and film posters, pictures loaned or bequeathed by members. The 50s clientele consists of queer gentlemen who tend to be arty, bohemian and well-heeled. Tradition has it that each night hospitality is extended by some of the members to soldiers, sailors, airmen and young men of no fixed reputation or fanciful dreams of gay social climbing

At the glamorous art deco cocktail bar, Brian, a camp barman in a blue blazer with hair nonchalantly swept back, busily makes up a variety of sophisticated or lurid cocktails. This is Vera's area, an ante-room where her favourites gather and through which members pass to the main piano bar, a large drinking area from which emanates a murmur of gentlemanly voices. Glenn Miller's "In the Mood" is being played. R are the steps that have led the way up to this roof-top club. There is a mirror behind the bar, and several tables surrounded by chairs

Vera, the owner of Queen Mab's, dressed with a louchely dramatic emphasis, too much jewellery and too little cosmetic restraint, mocks

*herself and the world with relish. She dances with Daniel in a would-be,
won't-be clinch. Both of them are a little sozzled*

Vera You're quite sweeping me off my feet.
Daniel No kidding? Where we off to?
Vera My lost youth of course.
Daniel Who's he?
Vera I never relied on a single beau.
Brian No. She spread herself around — and around.
Vera (*across to Brian*) At least, I'm not still spreading myself — unlike
  some I could mention, Brian Mandeville. I know how to play my
  age.
Brian Yes, dear — but you don't like to act it.
Vera (*clasping Daniel*) Oh, you're quite wasted on men!
Daniel Heck yes! I've wasted myself on far too many.
Vera (*to Daniel*) I just hope London's got you in its grip.
Daniel Sure. I'm gripped. Done with America!
Vera (*astonished, bringing the dancing to a halt*) I don't believe it. You
  had such a lovely war over here. All those stripes! All those soldiers
  under you!
Daniel (*sitting down at a table*) You can't be a faggot and work for the
  American government now.
Vera (*returning behind the bar*) But we had all those queer GIs in
  Mab's. Crew cuts, nice manners and loads of cash. (*She brings over a
  cocktail for Daniel*)
Daniel Yes but America's got the Cold War heebee-jeebees. They say
  faggots drop their pants for dreamboat Russian spies, get blackmailed
  and give away Yankee secrets.
Vera Isn't that's what your communists do?
Daniel (*raising his glass*) Nah. Reds don't drop their pants. They give
  away secrets for nothing. We're rated the big security risk.
Vera (*shaking her head*) It doesn't seem right to me, darling.
Daniel Nor me. So I gotta find a life here.
Vera But what will you do?
Daniel (*shrugging his shoulders*) I'll write or something ——
Vera Drown your sorrows in a Pink Lady for now, dear.

A buzzer sounds

Brian (*answering a phone*) Yes. Yes. Straight up! All the way. If you'll
  pardon my French.

From next door a singer with piano: they listen to the words

Singer (*off*)   I'm pretty, I'm witty, I'm queer.
                          I'm abusing myself with a strapping young peer.
                          He's there like a shot — if his girl's out of sight.
                          Oh you can't beat a lord
                          When it comes to delight in the night.

Vera You heard of this Lord Montagu they're singing about?

Daniel Nope.

Vera In the *Standard* tonight he is. Loitering in Paris! Due to be charged with a serious offence.

Daniel Which?

Brian The one a man does behind another man's back.

Daniel I thought that was gossip?

Vera No, dear, it's buggery.

Matthew enters, and stands embarrassed in the doorway

Good-evening, sir. May I help?

Daniel Hey. (*He raises his hand to Matthew*) Vera, this is my buddy Matt.

Vera Hallo, darling. I'm Miss Vera Dromgoole. Mab's own Queen. (*She holds out a majestic hand*)

Matthew shakes Vera's hand

And that's my Mistress of Ceremonies, Brian Mandeville.

Brian Hallo, darling! What's your pleasure.

Vera Five shillings for guest membership, Matt. Sign the book, sweetheart, for Brian. You can make up a name and an address.

Matthew goes over to the cocktail bar. Brian helps him

Matthew Oh thanks.

Vera Do French Ladies appeal to you, darling?

Matthew (*warily*) I'm not sure.

Daniel It's a cocktail. Bit too dramatic for you, Matt. He's happy with white wine.

Matthew returns to sit down with Daniel

Vera Bottle of Queen Mab's ordinaire, Brian. (*To Daniel*) Haven't you got yourself a nice, cheap friend, darling?

Brian walks out to the piano bar for supplies

Daniel Young men! One never counts the cost.

Vera Don't I know it! Now that Lord Montagu — he must be counting. Having boy scouts in his country home, he did. That's risky.

Daniel I was a boy scout once. It's OK in tents at night.

Vera Well, these ones were camping.

Daniel Fine and dandy.

Vera As for that Miss Baden-Powell! Stopping his scouts from a little light wanking. Dressing them in short trousers and woggles! Sending them out on bob-a-job week. Asking them to do their best for God. It's just not natural.

Daniel I had high times with scouts.

Vera Well, that sounds very right and improper.

Matthew The papers said they were acting as guides for his stately home.

Vera Scouts dressed as girl guides. Where will it all end?

Brian returns with the wine

Brian In a nasty court case. And us queens will get more nervous about cruising and having a gay flirt. (*He pours out the wine for Matthew*) This should put lead in your propelling pencil.

Matthew The police are gunning for famous queers.

Vera I wouldn't be surprised. It's not just your vicars and waiters these days up in court.

Daniel (*mock seriously*) You mean everyone's doing it?

Vera Yes. It's spreading. A novelist — jailed for taking two sailors home for hanky panky. An MP caught cruising Piccadilly Circus.

Brian moves back behind the bar

Who was he, Brian? His name was on everyone's lips.

Brian Not in my circles it wasn't.

Vera High time you got your circle widened, then.

Brian I nearly did, Miss D. Last Sunday. Thanks to a young dish. At the *Strutting Cock*.

Vera (*angered*) You promised you'd never go near the *Cock* again.

Brian I was tempted, wasn't I? It's not my brain leads me on.

Vera (*reproachful*) You're not safe to be let out alone, you aren't.

Brian Suddenly coppers everywhere. One old queen fainted clean away. Took down all our particulars. Frightening.

Vera Next thing they'll be going after posh totty in here. (*To Daniel and Matthew*) My clientele's very superior. Frightened of blackmail.

Matthew Of course.

Vera I don't know. I should never have left the stage.

Brian You didn't, dear. It left you.

Vera It was that Binkie Beaumont ruined my career. (*To Daniel*) Him and the war. Did I ever tell you about *The Boy in My Bedroom*?

Daniel Sounds very familiar.

Vera (*undeterred*) What a tour! Summer 1939 ... Bognor Regis, Crewe, Scunthorpe, Grimsby. Cleethorpes. Golders Green Hippodrome. Cheers all the way! I was teetering, Daniel, on the verge of stardom, but Binkie wouldn't bring us in. The bastard. Come on, Brian.

Brian and Vera sing and dance a number

Chiltern Moncrieffe, a stately but dishevelled queen in arty clothes with a black eye, and John Gielgud enter and watch

Vera (*singing*)   I'm Katie the cook who used to be fast,
Though now I've slowed down,
My flirting's a thing of the past.
I've had boys in my bedroom too often before,
But now I've a plucky young corporal I truly adore.

Brian
Vera   } (*together, singing*)
Oh it's divine time, summer thirty-nine time.
We just know there's a chance of a fine time.

Brian (*singing*)   Don't let the war-clouds shadow the sun.
Give peace a chance. Mr Chamberlain, we're out for fun.

Chiltern Vera, dear heart! Look who I've brought you!

Vera (*giving a little scream of delight*) I don't believe it. Angels of Sodom and Gomorrah! Sir Johnnie G back at Mabs and that wicked witch of a theatre critic bringing up the rear! (*She advances, ignoring Chiltern*)

Chiltern, Brian and Daniel watch this reunion

Gielgud My dear Vera. How brave! I didn't know you still sang. How I remember that big, vibrating voice of yours. (*He holds out a hand*)

Vera clutches Gielgud's hand

What a pleasure to see you looking so well preserved.

Vera Preserved? You make me sound like a long-lost jar of pre-war prunes.

Gielgud Oh no, no, darling! The years fall away like — like autumn plums when I look at you ——

Vera (*a bit mollified*) At least I don't remind you of some sad root vegetable.

Gielgud Certainly not, Vera. There was always something of the exotic fruit about you.

Vera (*motioning Gielgud and Chiltern to a table next to Matthew and Dan*) Exotic! I suppose I am in a way. Oh, Sir John. You know just how to flatter a girl.

Chiltern We're dining nearby — so I said let's slip into Mab's for old time's sake.

Vera Whisk up two Between the Sheets for the gentlemen, Brian. With a touch of pink in them.

Brian A couple of very stiff cocktails coming up.

Vera (*standing by them*) It's just like a dream. Why've you given us the cold shoulder so long, Sir John?

Gielgud Oh, Vera, one has to be careful. I can't be seen in dubious locations. No shady *boîte* for me. Such a pity! Should I even be here?

Vera How can you say, Sir John! Mab's is so refined these days — not like when you was here in nineteen forty-five ——

Gielgud Yes, yes, Vera, we won't delve into my past. It's far better left well behind me.

Chiltern That's true ——

Vera But now they've made a knight of you ——

Gielgud Sadly no one wants to make even half a night of me these days.

Vera Well we can't expect much at our age, can we?

Gielgud Indeed. I'm Miss Left-on-the-shelf these days.

Brian is cocktailing; Gielgud's attention is caught

Well — Brian still as naughty as ever, I hope.

Brian Oh my wickedness comes and goes, Sir John.

Vera That's the trouble. Brian meets danger half-way and gives him the nod. (*Her attention is taken by Chiltern*) Chiltern. Where did you get that black eye?

Chiltern The location is beside the point. I was set upon.

Vera Not by an actor I hope. I know they're vicious with critics. But it's usually done behind your backs.

Chiltern (*quietly*) It was an uncalled-for attack.

Vera Oh dearie me.

Brian comes round from behind the bar with the gawdy looking cocktails

Gielgud (*deflecting Vera's attention*) Now, now, Vera, wouldn't you introduce us to these delightful young men? Chiltern and I rarely have the chance to savour the cream of youth.

Vera Oh, Sir John! Always an eye for a friendly stranger! (*She gestures*) This is Daniel Arlington. He was a GI over here. And that's Matthew Barnsbury — his companion tonight. (*She walks back to the bar*)

There is a formal shaking of hands

Chiltern (*shaking hands with Daniel*) One always meets such an intriguing collection in Mab's.
Daniel Sure do.

There is the sound of laughter and applause from the piano bar

Gielgud I feel like a questing butterfly, Mr Barnsbury — not knowing on which flower to settle.

Matthew smiles in bemusement

Chiltern More like a dazzled moth, John. In danger of getting its wings singed.
Gielgud Butterflies get all the fun, I'm told.

A song begins next door. They listen

Voice (*singing; off*)
> Hi, there, young soldier boy. You look lonesome tonight.
> I'd throw you a line, but I'm not sure you'd bite.
> Black-outs and bombers have made us all nervous
> Oh God and our boys in the skies, please help preserve us.
> Oh, with you I'll get frisky on whisky,
> Or divine on red wine.
> So hand me a stiff one and we'll make it all night.

Applause

Gielgud What an embarrassment of nostalgia. (*To Daniel*) You GIs. What relief you brought us in our darkest hours. And packaged in such alluring uniforms too.
Daniel Yeah. We were quite well dressed. And undressed too.
Gielgud GIs had such a generous disposition — and so much to give.
Chiltern Now, now, John!
Daniel Yeah. Cigarettes, Hershey bars, chewing gum, Life Savers, genitalia and plenty of VD.
Gielgud Every pleasure has its price. One has to take the rough for the sake of the rough and tumble.

Chiltern (*drinking*) Life Savers and candy bars. The Yanks are coming. And you did at a stroke, Mr Arlington. Not you personally of course ——

Daniel blushes charmingly and smiles

Vera GIs always ready for a bit of what you fancy — but dearie me! They didn't last long. (*To Daniel*) Though you weren't like that, darling, were you?

Daniel blushes again

Gielgud Happy days! Or rather nights — when they weren't bombing! Hermione Gingold's dressing room. VE night. She'd filthy finger nails and three delicious GIs. So greedy. She insisted on keeping two for herself.
Matthew What happened to the third?

They look at him. Laughter

Gielgud He was very well cared for, Mr Barnsbury!
Brian I remember one black-out night ——
Vera Really — Brian, Sir John doesn't want a guided tour down that grim little cul-de-sac you call your memory lane.
Gielgud Oh. But I do. It's nice to be a guided voyeur at my age.
Chiltern (*warning*) Careful, John! What brings you back to London, Mr Arlington?
Daniel Lost my job.
Chiltern I'm so sorry. How's that?
Daniel (*shaking his head*) I was set for the Embassy here. But now they've got it in for queers. They made me take a lie detector. I was kicked out.
Gielgud (*shocked*) Is it as simple as that?
Daniel Sure. Federal government — they're clearing perverts out faster and faster. Hundreds a month.
Gielgud Thank God we do things differently.
Chiltern Well I've heard of the odd resignation ——
Matthew (*suddenly*) It's happening in London too. It's all done quietly behind the scenes.
Gielgud Oh no, I doubt it.
Matthew I'm afraid so.
Daniel How would you know, Matt?

Silence

Matthew I'm afraid it's confidential. I shouldn't say.

This causes consternation

Daniel (*standing up*) You get more interesting every minute, Matt. Come to the piano bar. Let's have a quiet chat in there.
Matthew All right. (*He stands up too. Generally*) I'm sorry — I wanted to warn ——

This causes a frisson of anxiety

Daniel Come on, Matt.
Chiltern Good-night, Mr Barnsbury. Don't apologize.
Daniel (*as they go*) Vera! Gentlemen!

Daniel and Matthew exit

Brian That Matthew! Get her! Who does she think she is?
Chiltern Someone with his finger on the pulse. Frightening!
Gielgud Such handsome young men! I suppose they're entwined. My fantasies go with them.
Chiltern (*mopping his eye with his handkerchief*) Yes — well, as long as you leave it at fantasizing. This American panic over queers. Our political correspondent — he'll give me the accurate story. My eye hurts! (*He gets up and goes over to the bar mirror to examine his eye*)

Brian joins Chiltern

Gielgud (*aside to Vera*) Poor Chiltern. Such unsuitable longings. His regular guardsman. Violent. Stole his watch. Took fifty pounds.
Vera Where's decency gone these days? (*She goes to rummage behind the bar*)
Gielgud (*shaking his head*) I've never kept track of it, I'm afraid.

Chiltern returns and sits down. Vera comes over with witch hazel and a cloth

Chiltern It looks most unseemly.
Vera Let's try witch hazel, darling. (*She dabs the sides of his eye*)
Chiltern Ah. "*Ce n'est plus un ardeur dans les veins caches. C'est Venus toute entiere a sa proie attaché.*"
Vera Yes, bloody Venus! She's got a lot to answer for.

Chiltern "It's not the hots that I've got. Passion's sunk its teeth into me like a mad dog and won't let go." Racine.

Vera Whoever she is!

Chiltern I always thought the pleasurable thing about being a theatre critic ——

Gielgud (*lightly*) Something faintly indecent about a reviewer taking pleasure in himself.

Chiltern But now the cold douche of reality ——

Vera I suppose ice wouldn't help, dear?

Chiltern (*shaking his head*) Should we glance into the piano bar? (*He looks at his watch*) Oh dear. It's later than I thought. We must go.

Gielgud Vera, Brian. This has been an enchanting trip to *temps perdu*.

Vera comes out from the cocktail bar. Gielgud kisses her. Chiltern sits lost in thought

Vera Don't be a stranger again, Sir John.

Gielgud Chiltern. Come!

Chiltern stands, disconsolate

We all fall from grace to disgrace one way or another. When Venus forces us into unbecoming positions, we just have to smile, keep our nerve and put on an act.

Gielgud and Chiltern walk out

Brian Well, Miss God's got a lot to answer for!

Vera returns to the bar

Vera (*picking up a tray to exit*) Don't be silly, dear. She's not in direct control.

SCENE 9

A room at the Polynaeum, an ancient club in Pall Mall furnished in late Victorian style. It is a place where top gentlemen can have a drink in private together before dinner. The ancient Lord Chief Justice Lord Goddard, a man not afraid to look ghastliness in a glare of outrage, sits reading a book. He has a glass of sherry by his side. He speaks with all the leisurely confidence of a horse-drawn royal carriage trotting towards its destination

A distraught Mr Justice Lightbourne rushes in, in his late forties and wearing a coat. Hat in hand. This High Court Judge looks lean, long and as immaculate as a well-folded umbrella. His features are reminiscent of a middle-aged cherub. He distils a courteous detachment, a studied politesse. His eyes are swimming pool blue

Lightbourne Apologies — this lateness — sir. Very few taxis.

Goddard gets himself up. He holds out a hand to be shaken and claps Lightbourne paternally on the back

Goddard Percy, my boy. Never mind. This is a treat and a half. Sink your good self into the plush.

Goddard and Lightbourne shake hands. They remain standing

Yes. Grim times. Let me put a reviving beverage in that firm hand of yours. Where's Witherby? (*He presses a button*) Witherby! Where the devil is he? Bloody tanker-drivers ...
Lightbourne Of course it's an unofficial strike.
Goddard Well they've gone too far this time ... The Home Secretary's delayed. Organizing a nice little State of Emergency.
Lightbourne Oh dear.
Goddard David's very eager to meet you. He's due any second.
Lightbourne To think he wants to see me.
Goddard Not at all. Likes to meet the odd high court judge ...
Lighbourne How kind!
Goddard I don't know, Percy — these Union leaders — used to be salt of the earth — with a bit of pepper to keep us on our toes. But now they're all swinging left. The decent working man — putty in their horny hands.
Lightbourne They say bread runs out in London tomorrow. How will the workers breakfast?
Goddard Let them eat humble pie ...

Witherby bustles in, his clothes transformed from his earlier lavatorial garb

Ah, Douglas, you've turned up at last.
Witherby Beg pardon, my Lord. There was an incident in the kitchens...
Goddard Never you mind. Got a good, dry sherry for Sir Percy?
Witherby I've a lovely Spanish number downstairs, my Lord. With a Bohemian bouquet.

Goddard (*jocularly*) That's the spirit, Douglas. A bit of the Spanish Bohemian.

Witherby exits

Talking of which, Percy — Bohemians that is — I saw your younger son at the theatre the other day.

Lightbourne (*startled*) He never mentioned ...

Goddard A first night. He seemed to be with a theatre critic.

Lightbourne I'm sure he wouldn't know one.

Goddard A large, flamboyant fellow. What's his name? Writes for that silly, liberal paper.

Lightbourne (*disturbed*) The *Morning View*? Chiltern Moncrieffe? Surely not.

Goddard Not quite the ticket is he?

Lightbourne I'm sure Gregory wouldn't be seen with him ...

Goddard I don't forget a face. (*Pause*) You don't know Moncrieffe?

Lightbourne Just slightly. At Oxford. He acted in the OUDS. Made an unseemly Mercutio ...

Witherby brings in sherry in a decanter and pours two glasses out for them

Goddard I once saw John Gielgud have a shot at Romeo. Rather disgusting I thought. Not enough balls. And to give him a knighthood!

Lightbourne He does rather let that voice of his run away with him.

Goddard You know Olivier begged Winston to give him the K.

Lightbourne Michael Redgrave. Now there's a proper actor!

Goddard But it's your own performance, Percy, that caught the Home Sec's attention ...

Lightbourne I can't think why.

Goddard You inspired such useful headlines over those Tunbridge Wells sodomists. He liked your angle.

Lightbourne I'm afraid I spoke from the heart ...

Goddard Quite right. It's a judge's vital organ. Not wise to leave it all to the brain cells ... "Top Judge Lashes Vice Wave Perverts." I like the *Daily Mail*'s cool way with headlines ... Usually top judges isn't it? Never bottom ones.

Lightbourne The proselytizers disturb me most. Coax a young fellow to deviate — and you've often turned him for life.

Goddard Quite so. My splendid usher was importuned in a municipal swimming pool only last week. And he's fifty-three.

Lightbourne (*bemused by the old man's thought-ramble*) These new hormonal therapies ——

Goddard (*benign, but shaking his head*) Too expensive. Fear. That's the best deterrent. And kindest.

Lightbourne Is it possible to terrorize people into being lawful?

Goddard I warned the Labour government there'd be trouble when they abolished the cat o' nine tails. And now the Tories are afraid to bring it back. Look at London now — teeming with cosh-boys, knuckle dusters and juveniles hoping to become delinquent.

Lightbourne (*dubiously*) I don't think fear works as a moral form of deterrent.

Goddard Ah, morals have to come second! George the Fifth. He had the right idea.

Lightbourne (*resigned; he has heard the story before*) Oh, really!

Goddard "Flog 'em, Goddard," he whispered. I was on my knees at the time. He was knighting me. There was a man!

Witherby enters, excited

Witherby Oh, my Lord! The Home Secretary. Passing through the foyer now. Members applauding him.

The sounds of applause eddy through the open door

Goddard Capital. Thank you, Douglas.

Witherby exits

Goddard and Lightbourne stand up

The sound of applause and voices shouting "Bravo, sir" reach them

Maxwell Fyfe, the firm, right-wing moralist, arrives

Fyfe Gentlemen! Good evening. Apologies. We may have a state of emergency tomorrow.

Goddard David, my boy — what a serious pleasure. Just you go for those strikers. We're behind you.

Fyfe and Goddard shake hands

And here's Percy Lightbourne.

Fyfe and Lightbourne shake hands

Lightbourne Delighted to meet you, sir.

Fyfe Percy, how are you? Never fear, Rayner. We'll bring these petrol tanker drivers to their senses — or their knees.

Goddard They'll come to their senses — show them who're the masters now ...

Fyfe (*melancholic*) We've not enough grip for that these days, Rayner. World gets more dangerous daily. Which way for Russia now Stalin's gone, I ask myself. London's packed with their spies. We're dabbling with H-bombs. My civil servants make doomsday scenarios for fear of a nuclear hit. It doesn't make for sunny days in Whitehall.

Goddard With your firm hand on the tiller at home, David, I sleep soundly each night.

Witherby enters with sherry for Fyfe. He fills the glasses of the other two men while they talk, then exits

Fyfe (*to Lightbourne*) Now, Percy — you'll be interested. D'you know my brother-in-law, Rex Harrison?

Lightbourne I've always admired his light comic touch.

Goddard Now he acted with that corking actress. 1930s. Never forget her. Name's on tip of my tongue ...

Fyfe "Warn your queer pals in the Green Room," I said to Rex ... "Tell them I'm going to eliminate homosexuality."

Lightbourne (*disturbed*) Eliminate?

Fyfe The practice not the practitioners. You might as well try to stamp out the common cold, he said. Just you watch, Rex, I answered.

Goddard Jessica. Jessica Tandy. (*Singing*)
> And what could be better, if only they'd let her
> Come out for a night on the town,
> Then I'd gladly go down,
> For a bit of a fling with Miss Jessica Tandy.

Those were the days!

Fyfe (*bemused by Goddard*) Now, Percy — we're on Privy Council terms. America's taking a new stiff line on the inversion problem. Not just reds in your bed these days. Blackmailable homos too.

Lightbourne Of course.

Fyfe Interesting figures ... In five months about two thousand of their federal workers got kicked out or resigned. Most of them queer security risks.

Goddard There's a clean up!

Fyfe Obviously we do that sort of thing behind the scenes. Now America wants to see us a bit more vigilant about queers in the diplomatic service.

Lightbourne Perfectly understandable!

Fyfe This upcoming Montagu case — that'll serve notice — but we've had a stroke of good luck.

Goddard DPP knows a trick or two.

Fyfe We've a sweep for queers in the military ... Search of lockers in the Far East. They had a find. Letters linking two young airmen, with Montagu and his cronies. Surprising?

Lightbourne I don't really know.

Fyfe Chance is the DPP can persuade the airmen to turn Queen's Evidence. So even if Montagu's found innocent we then hope to do our young peer for queer conspiracy.

Lightbourne But he wouldn't have the chance of a fair trial surely?

Fyfe That's not what the DPP tells me.

Lightbourne It sounds legally doubtful to me.

Fyfe Come, Percy. You judges don't object when police search a queer's house without search warrants. You don't object when they're denied access to a solicitor.

Lightbourne But I don't like it.

Fyfe We've penetrated a homosexual network in the armed services. It's a security matter now.

Lightbourne I see.

Fyfe What I'm hoping for — once we've had this first Montagu trial — is that a few judges will be minded to call for a national campaign against male vice.

Lightbourne Ah!

Fyfe Of course you hit the nail on the head last week with your Tunbridge Wells judgment.

Lightbourne What would this campaign do?

Fyfe It would help me in cabinet — colleagues agitating for Royal Commissions and so forth. All too lengthy and uncivilized — if you expressed an opinion ... Very useful for me.

Lightbourne A national campaign — sounds very promising. Psychiatry and medical treatment ... It's the inverts who prey upon young men, wreck their lives — they're the crucial ones.

Goddard That's the spirit.

Lightbourne Hospital treatment not prison.

Fyfe Oh no! Out of the question. Too expensive. The public would be outraged.

Lightbourne Then they must be educated. This is a moral emergency.

Fyfe Mothers and fathers want to protect their sons, Percy. It's a natural family feeling isn't it?

Lightbourne (*quietly*) But some of their sons are coaxed into homosexuality ... They have fathers and mothers too. We ought to be protecting them. That's crucial if we're to have change for the better.

Fyfe Let me explain, Percy. We're basically on the same side. I know that.

Goddard Champagne please, Witherby. At the double!

Witherby brings in champagne

Goddard A toast!

Witherby pops the cork of the champagne. He serves the drinks as Fyfe speaks. He exits after having poured the drinks

Fyfe (*gently*) Sending them to gaol — that's the best way to stop their proselytising and seducing. We'll clear them from pubs, clubs and public spaces. It'll be discreetly done. Their power to corrupt the young will diminish. I've a dream that homosexuality will be dying out. (*Raising his glass*) A toast for our campaign. You'll notice the champagne's the right colour — none of that disturbing pink stuff for us!

Goddard Come, dinner awaits us. Percy. Youngsters first ——

Lightbourne leads the way, and exits

Fyfe (*aside to Goddard; shaking his head*) He won't do, Rayner. He won't.

Fyfe and Goddard exit

SCENE 10

St James's Park

Back projections show midnight views of St James's Park wreathed in the 1950s mists of October. Trees are laden with autumnal leaves. Figures stand as if frozen on pathways lit faintly by gaslight. Distant prospect of Buckingham Palace

Gielgud and Chiltern walk on, pause as if they have reached the point where they part. They are both a bit drunk

Gielgud Coriolanus! Never! The role's far too butch for me ... All that fighting! Macbeth was bad enough.

Chiltern But you've got the right arrogance. There's that queer business in Aufidius. And you used to have muscular legs.

Gielgud (*looking down*) Strange! The muscles are still there — the one thing about me that made Larry jealous. Anyway I'm too indecisive to be arrogant.

Chiltern (*gazing at the park*) Guardsmen, I'm sure. Trying to get up to no good, I hope.

Gielgud Careful, Chiltern. No wandering. You don't want any fresh assault upon your person.

Chiltern My dear John. You know I'm not prone to put myself out for public tender.

Gielgud Ah! But one never knows when temptation will get the better of us ...

Chiltern You speak for yourself.

Gielgud Now those Hollywood extra boys when I was filming *Julius Caesar*. Any of them would have melted in my mouth.

Chiltern That frightful mousetrap cheese they gave us — it still clings to my palate.

Gielgud Charity, Chiltern. Food rationing stumps all but the best cooks. And we had rhubarb crumble after all.

Chiltern (*still distracted by the park*) Why don't people just arrange to have them come back home? So much safer.

Gielgud Not in your case!

Chiltern This has been my first mishap. In twenty-five years.

Gielgud What a long run you've had. But it only goes to show ...

Chiltern I must say I was terrified by what they said at dinner about their old friend.

Gielgud Which one? (*He too is gazing into the park*) I can see vague figures now. Such a romantic setting — all shadows, falling leaves and upright gentlemen poised to stoop to conquer.

Chiltern The one who chose hormone therapy instead of prison and developed women's breasts.

Gielgud What a barbarous world it is! And his balls shrunk to the size of raspberries. I certainly won't be able to eat that over-rated fruit again. I mustn't dawdle. A last run-through tomorrow. Oh, dear!

Chiltern Is it not up to par?

Gielgud Ralph's bound to steal the show. He always makes such an amusing drunk.

Chiltern Well, no time for regrets.

Gielgud No.

Chiltern   (*holding out a hand*) Good-night, my dear John. Straight
home! No loitering, no deviating from the straight and narrow ...

Gielgud and Chiltern shake hands

Gielgud   Deviation's the last thing on my mind after that terrible balls
and breast story ... Good-night.

  Chiltern walks away

*Gielgud stands there. He removes his tie and then brings out a cap from
his inside jacket pocket and puts it on his head*

  Gielgud walks briskly into the darkness which swallows him up

                              SCENE 11

The Dudmaston Mews public lavatory

*A spotlight on Gielgud, lighting a cigarette. There is the sound of latrine
waters*

*Beams of light focus on the lavatories. Gielgud walks briskly in and goes
straight to the urinals. He is smoking. Greg, lengthily washing his hands
and loitering by the wash basin, shoots a glance of recognition at him.
Gielgud pays no attention. He urinates. He does not rinse his hands.
They were less hygiene-prone in those days. Gielgud goes to exit*

*Terry walks in. He stares at Gielgud who meets his look with a smile.
Both walk on. Gielgud turns back, so does Terry. They hold each other
in a gaze. Terry goes to the urinal. Gielgud turns back and goes towards
the urinal. He stands at a distance watching. Greg watches. Gielgud
watches. Terry winks at Gielgud. Gielgud takes a small tentative step
forward. There must be nothing dramatic or threatening about his slight
movement. Terry leaps to arrest Gielgud*

Terry   (*producing a police identity card; he gets Gielgud in an
  elbow-hold*) OK. Police. You're nicked.
Gielgud   I don't understand. What d'you think I've done? I was only
  urinating.
Greg   He didn't do anything. (*To Gielgud*) I'll be your witness. (*To
  Terry*) You're arresting an innocent man.

Terry Just you keep out of this, sonny.
Greg You've set him up.
Terry (*to Greg*) You piss off or I'll have you for obstructing a police officer! (*To Gielgud*) You'll be taken to a police station and charged with persistently importuning male persons for immoral purposes.
Gielgud Oh, no!

Terry releases Gielgud from the elbow-hold. Greg watches

Terry Oh yes!
Gielgud I'm terribly sorry.
Terry Sorry? You don't have to be sorry for me, sir. I'm just doing my job. What's your name?
Gielgud I didn't do anything.
Terry That'll be for the courts to decide.
Gielgud Please! I've been out. I've had a few drinks.
Greg (*stepping forward*) This is a set-up. He didn't do anything.

Terry blows his police whistle. Gielgud looks helplessly at Greg

Terry (*suddenly overwhelmed*) I'm sorry. There's nothing I can do. Really sorry.

There is the sound of Bellinger's footsteps. Greg moves swiftly into a cubicle

Bellinger appears

Bellinger What's happening then, Constable?
Terry (*gesturing towards Gielgud*) I've arrested him for persistently importuning, Inspector Bellinger.
Bellinger Very good. Carry on then, Constable. (*He watches*)
Terry What's your name?
Gielgud Gielgud. Arthur Gielgud.
Terry (*getting out notebook*) Gielgud. That's a funny one. You don't sound like a foreigner.
Gielgud No. Not me. Just the name.

Pause

Terry How d'you spell it?
Gielgud G - I - E - L - G - U - D.
Terry Address?

Gielgud Sixteen Cowley Street, SW1.
Terry Profession?
Gielgud Clerk.
Terry Age?
Gielgud Forty-nine.
Terry Don't worry, sir. It's not too big a fine.
Gielgud But I … the publicity.
Terry Publicity. There won't be any for the likes of you.
Gielgud Will I be put in a cell?
Bellinger The press couldn't give a toss for your ordinary working man, Mr Gielgud. They're interested in lords and vicars, scoutmasters and MPs caught in urinals.

Terry takes out handcuffs

Gielgud Do you have to put those on me?
Bellinger Regulations, Mr Gielgud. I'm sorry. You might make a run for it. (*He takes the handcuffs from Terry*)
Gielgud How absurd!
Bellinger Now Mr Gielgud, we're off to Chelsea police station where you'll be formally charged. All right, Constable?
Terry There's another one, Steve. A young chap. (*He gestures towards the cubicle*)
Bellinger Committing an offence?
Terry Just watching, Steve.
Bellinger That's nasty. You deal with him. (*He goes to handcuff Gielgud*)
Gielgud Oh, no! This can't be.
Bellinger I don't suppose you've been handcuffed before, Mr Gielgud?

Gielgud shakes his head

You'll be all right, just as long as you're sensible.
Gielgud Sensible?
Bellinger I can see you're an intelligent man. It's in your interests to plead guilty.
Gielgud But I didn't do anything.
Bellinger Persistent importuning. Clever offence. It's not what you do, it's what you signal you want to do.
Gielgud I didn't give a signal.
Bellinger Better plead guilty, Mr Gielgud. All over quickly. No waiting months for a jury trial. Never know what would come out in court under cross-examination.

Gielgud I understand.
Bellinger We always try to help in the police service. Right, Mr Gielgud!
    Let's get those handcuffs on you, sharpish.

Gielgud holds out his hands

    That's the way. (*Putting handcuffs on*) They're a snug fit.

Bellinger and Gielgud exit

Terry Police! Come on out. (*He stands back and waits*)

*Greg comes out, stands there. Silence for a moment. They size each
other up*

Greg I'm allowed to use the lavatory.
Terry Why you hanging around then?

Silence

Greg I've done nothing. He was only standing there.
Terry You know you shouldn't be doing this.
Greg What?
Terry Come on. You know the odds. No loitering. No looking. How
    old are you?
Greg I'll be nineteen soon.
Terry Streuth.
Greg What d'you mean?
Terry At your age!

Silence

Greg You've gone and ruined someone famous.
Terry Him famous? He's a clerk.
Greg He's not a clerk. He's John Gielgud.
Terry Who's John Gielgud?
Greg Have you never been to a theatre?
Terry I've been to *South Pacific*.
Greg He's a great actor.
Terry Don't look like one of them to me.
Greg They made him a knight for his acting.
Terry Blimey! (*Silence*) How d'you know who he is?

Pause

Greg I've seen him. On stage.

They stand there looking at each other. Something is understood

Terry You don't want to have to be cautioned, do you?
Greg Oh, no! (*Pause*) Please ——
Terry (*change of tone*) D'you think I like doing this?

Silence

Greg I hope not. No! I don't think you do.
Terry What's your name then?
Greg Greg.
Terry Well! (*Pause*) I'll be keeping an eye out for you, Greg.
Greg (*fighting with himself over what move he should make, if any*)
   Where?

Pause

Terry I'm taking a risk with you, aren't I?
Greg (*shaking his head*) No.
Terry I don't want to find you in here again.
Greg (*quietly*) Where would you want to find me then?

Terry looks at him

   Please — couldn't you try to get him off. Please.
Terry Out of my hands. You live local then?
Greg Chelsea.
Terry I know Chelsea. You do any swimming?
Greg Sometimes.
Terry Well I never. I'm in the Chelsea pool myself. Saturday. Afternoons.
   After three ... Might bump into you there. Very soon.
Greg Yes. Yes I'll be there then. Thanks.
Terry OK — Greg.

   Terry walks out

Gielgud's home

Two in the morning, hours after his arrest and after he has been bailed. Gielgud sits at a writing desk. His face betrays by its listlessness the symptoms of shock. He has struggled to compose himself. He does not weep but tears trickle down his face. He sits staring into space. He trembles. A grandfather clock strikes two. Chiltern paces

Gielgud I said I was a clerk. A clerk! Why did I do that, Chiltern?

Chiltern Tell me how it happened.

Gielgud (*dragging out the words as if they cost him physical pain*) You see they took me to the station. I was handcuffed. (*He holds up his hands*) Very tight. They took me into this room. They weren't pleasant. I've been charged. I ... (*He shakes his head*) I'm up in court tomorrow morning.

Chiltern I suppose they got you in a cottage?

Gielgud nods

Oh, John — what were you doing?

Gielgud It was this young policeman.

Chiltern Surely you recognize what they look like?

Gielgud He was coming in. I was going out. He stared at me. I smiled. I followed him back.

Chiltern That's all?

Gielgud I stood there. The urinal. At a distance.

Chiltern Yes?

Gielgud He winked. He grabbed hold of me. I'm finished.

Chiltern You've phoned your solicitor?

Gielgud I don't think I have one.

Chiltern We'll phone Binkie. He knows how to square the police.

Gielgud Oh, I couldn't ... I'm too ashamed. (*He wipes his face. He shakes his head again*)

Chiltern I can get my solicitor.

Gielgud I'm pleading guilty. Say I'd drunk one too many. Didn't know what I was doing.

Chiltern I don't know if that's right.

Gielgud A guilty plea — avoids a full trial.

Chiltern I wonder — can they convict you — on a smile and a few steps?

Gielgud Of course. They can invent anything. Magistrates always believe them.

Chiltern Our police are notoriously corrupt. They can be bought, thank
God.

Gielgud If the press get hold of the story ——

Chiltern Binkie could buy them off. He's very close to Anthony Eden.

Gielgud (*shaking his head*) I could even go to prison.

Chitlern Not for a bit of importuning.

Gielgud Oh, yes. Max Adrian got six months. In the war.

Chiltern Where was he? Italy? Yugoslavia?

Gielgud Victoria Station. (*Flicker of amusement*) The line is immaterial.
(*Pause*) I've let everyone down.

Chiltern That's the least of it now ——

Gielgud My doctor's coming to court with me. A little moral support.

Chiltern But rehearsals. Without you?

Gielgud I'll get a message to Binkie. (*Pause*) I'll invent an excuse.
Teeth! A raging toothache.

Chiltern Please tell him the truth. It won't come as that great a
surprise...

Gielgud What d'you mean?

Chiltern He knows about you.

Gielgud How could he?

Chiltern Johnnie, how could he not? People know about you ——

Gielgud How stupid I've been.

The phone rings

Who can that be?

Chiltern You'd better answer.

Gielgud (*on the phone*) Hullo ... Who? ... Yes, that's me! (*Pause. He
listens*) Yes. You're right. Arthur's my first name ... Yes, yes. That's
very good of you indeed ... Thank you ... Of course I would! Thank
you! Nine o'clock ... I'll be there. Of course. Goodbye. (*He puts the
phone down*) Thank goodness.

Chiltern What's happened?

Gielgud The desk sergeant. So helpful. He guessed who I am.

Chiltern Doesn't sound good to me.

Gielgud They can get me seen by the early magistrate. Before the court
reporters start. There won't be any press, thank God.

West London Magistrates' court

A searchlight now begins to beam all round the empty stage and settles on John Gielgud. He stands

Voice Tell the court your name.
Gielgud Arthur John Gielgud.
Voice Address?
Gielgud Sixteen Cowley Street. SW1.
Voice Occupation?
Gielgud Clerk.
Voice Are you employed?
Gielgud Self-employed.
Voice Age?
Gielgud Forty-nine.
Voice Arthur Gielgud. You are charged with persistently importuning male persons for immoral purposes at Dudmaston Mews, Chelsea, on the night of October the twenty-first. How do you plead?
Gielgud Guilty.
Voice Have you anything to say?
Gielgud (*facing him*) I cannot imagine I was so stupid. I was tired and had had a few drinks. I was not responsible for my actions.
Magistrate (*voice off*) If this is what you do when you have taken more drinks than you are able to control, you would be a wise man if you drank less. See your doctor the moment you leave here and tell him. If he has any advice to offer, take it, because your conduct is dangerous to other men, particularly to young men, and is a scourge in this neighbourhood. I have something like six hundred of these cases every year and I begin think they should all be sent to prison as they were in the old days — when there were fewer of them. I suppose on this occasion I can treat you as a bad case of drunk and disorderly, but nobody can do that again. You will be fined ten pounds.

Gielgud walks out

Outside the Haymarket Theatre. Evening

An evening newspaper vendor stand. There is an "Evening Standard" placard which reads "GIELGUD FINED FOR VICE OFFENCE"

Bert the news vendor cries out

Bert STAR! NEWS! STANDARD! GIELGUD SENSATION! GUILTY ON VICE OFFENCE!

Binkie Beaumont and Sybil Thorndike enter, strolling towards the theatre after a leisurely lunch. Binkie carries an umbrella and wears a trilby

Binkie (*seeing the placard*) Oh my God! (*He stops in his tracks*)

Sybil can't read the placard without her spectacles

Binkie goes over to Bert

Hallo, Bert. (*He pays his one and a halfpenny for a copy*)
Bert Hello, sir. Dame Sybil. Bit of trouble for you, I'm afraid, Mr Beaumont.
Binkie Thank you, Bert. (*He looks at the front page, moving away from Bert*)
Sybil (*following him*) Binkie — I don't understand! What's John done?
Binkie Rather too much. (*He shows Sybil the headline*) Fined. Persistently importuning. A public lavatory.
Sybil Oh, no. Surely he wouldn't be so indiscreet. (*She rummages in her bag for spectacles. She retrieves them and reads the offending placard and the "Evening Standard" report*)
Binkie I'm afraid so. He pleaded guilty.
Sybil But how vulgar to give it all this publicity.
Binkie Sells papers.
Sybil Poor John! People will be so shocked.
Binkie Yes — but how will theatregoers react?
Bert STAR! NEWS! STANDARD! GIELGUD SENSATION! GUILTY ON VICE OFFENCE!
Binkie (*irritated; going over to Bert*) Bert. Sir John will be back with us shortly. Coming by taxi. It would be much nicer if he didn't have to hear you shouting the news out loud.

Bert Well, Mr Beaumont, I dunno. It's a big story. Nasty for you, Dame Sybil. Having to act with him.

Binkie (*extracting a five pound note from his wallet*) Yes, but they'll read the placards. If you could stop shouting about Sir John — just for the next hour ——

Bert (*taking the fiver*) Well, seeing as you ask — that's very generous, Mr Beaumont. Thank you, sir.

Binkie walks back to Sybil

Sybil To think he could do something so schoolboyish.
Binkie I'd like you to talk to the cast.
Sybil They'll have seen the placards.
Binkie Warn them not to say anything to John.
Sybil Of course. I'll put the fear of God in them.
Binkie If only someone had done that to John in time.
Sybil Couldn't you have, dear?
Binkie I'll see him first before he comes over to you. I really rather wonder ——
Sybil Will he have to leave us?
Binkie Who knows?

Sybil and Binkie walk out

As soon as they have gone Bert shouts

Bert STAR! NEWS! STANDARD! FAMOUS ACTOR GUILTY ON VICE CHARGE!

SCENE 15

Binkie Beaumont's office

There is an antique desk, equipped with one period telephone and a table-lamp. Binkie Beaumont, dressed with expensive tastefulness and elegantly coiffeured, is speaking into the telephone

Binkie He's on his way. (*In a languid, non-committal drawl*) Yes. Oh yes ... I wouldn't want to pay such a large sum ... Well! Fancy! ... Oh, if we can make a profit that's different. He's on his way. I'm having a board meeting at seven to consider the position. I'm in two minds. We may have to let him go. Would Alec be free to take over? Or even Paul?

Gielgud knocks at the door

Come in!

Gielgud enters

Let me know anyway. Goodbye. (*He looks up and sees Gielgud*) My dear, I was just talking about you. Can't say how sorry I am.

Gielgud Oh, it's not that bad. I'm taking strong painkillers.

Binkie (*bemused*) Really! Will they help somehow?

Gielgud Oh I need to — they yanked it out quite easily. But even so ——

Binkie John — you've obviously not seen the *Evening Standard*.

Gielgud Why? What's in it?

Binkie I'm afraid you are. On the front page too. (*He hands over the paper*)

Gielgud puts on glasses to read

Perhaps you'd like to tell me ——

Gielgud is visibly shocked

Yes, it's most unfortunate.

Gielgud (*aghast, putting the newspaper on the desk*) But they said there wouldn't be any press. (*Pause*) I was seen early.

Binkie (*producing a glass and a bottle of whisky from the bottom drawer of his desk and pouring out one measure*) You'll need a bit of a steadier.

Gielgud takes the whisky

Gielgud I'm finished. There must be a mistake.

Binkie You'd be a millionaire if there was one.

Gielgud I'm ruined.

Binkie A tricky situation, yes. Ruined? Certainly not! I suppose you were set up.

Gielgud I'd peed respectably. Dudmaston Mews. I was passing.

Binkie Ah!

Gielgud There was this young man coming in as I left. He stared at me ... he winked.

Binkie Ah the winkers, dear. Dangerous to let the eyes roam, in latrines or even on the streets.

Gielgud It all happened in a flash. I only smiled ——

Binkie A wink and a smile and a stare? Lethal combination.

Gielgud Yes.

Binkie Johnnie! A knight of the theatre — surely he avoids public lavatories like the plague. In emergencies he urinates in the gutter. Discreetly. The pretty police are always loitering with intent.

Gielgud (*shaking his head*) Yes. I've let you all down very badly. I can only apologize.

Binkie Your solicitor advised you to plead guilty?

Gielgud He wasn't with me. I didn't contact him.

Binkie (*amazed*) You weren't represented?

Gielgud My doctor came with me.

Binkie Whatever for? You weren't pleading the balance of your mind was disturbed.

Gielgud A little moral support ... they arranged to have me dealt with early — before the press start.

Binkie John, the police tip off Fleet Street when there's a famous arrest.

Gielgud Oh!

Binkie Did you think they wouldn't recognize you? Calling yourself a clerk. Not a good move.

Gielgud Yes.

Binkie Of course they wanted you in early. To give the *Evening Standard* a lunch-time exclusive. Ghastly little gossip sheet. They get paid.

Gielgud So that's why the desk sergeant was helpful.

Binkie Our policemen! What they'll do for money.

Gielgud I'm afraid I'm not familiar with them.

Binkie At least that's one danger averted. (*Pause*) Why didn't you phone me? They might have been paid off.

Gielgud I was ashamed.

Binkie You let me down not phoning.

Gielgud Yes. (*Pause*) Of course I'll have to leave the play.

Binkie Oh I don't know about that, dear. Mr Hunter's lovely new piece — we've the Haymarket opening in — what — six weeks? It can't be lightly tossed aside.

Gielgud How can I go on? I can't stay in the public eye.

Binkie People like to forgive stars if they can. You're adored. Anyway you're irreplaceable.

Gielgud But the public ——

Binkie Never mind them, dear. Leave them to me. I've told Sybil.

Gielgud How did she take it?

Binkie With tea and sympathy. Everyone's read the *Evening Standard* of course.

Gielgud (*shuddering*) How kind!

Binkie Buck up, dear. Sybil's spoken to everyone. She was a suffragette after all. She knows what it's like to be up against the law.

Gielgud Hers was a noble cause.

Binkie Man-handled by the police. Just like you.

Gielgud And Ralph? His thoughts on sex don't run very far from the straight and narrow ——

Binkie He's bemused. Puts it down to alcohol. He's distressed for you.

Gielgud Well I must face the music.

Binkie I can't believe this'll stop your lovely loyal public buying tickets.

Gielgud I thought we had a wonderful box office advance already.

Binkie We do. (*Jocularly*) But we can't rely on your advances, can we? Box office appeal — such a mysterious, fragile thing.

Gielgud I'm afraid I won't appeal to anyone any more.

Binkie If I were one of your middle-aged, lady admirers from Tunbridge Wells I'd be upset — right down to my thick, linen underwear, but I wouldn't give you up. Oh no.

Gielgud They'll be revolted.

Binkie They're far too nice to jump to the right conclusion.

Gielgud (*looking at the newspaper*) They've chosen such an unflattering photo. I look like Dracula prowling for the next vein.

Binkie The press won't resist a little blood-sucking in a good cause.

Gielgud (*after a pause*) They'll laugh me off stage and jeer. If I play Lear or Prospero they'll only remember my lavatorial debacle.

The phone rings

Binkie Oh no. People have such respectable minds these days. They'll much prefer to jump to the wrong conclusion. (*Into the telephone*) Yes? ... Oh, well I didn't expect we'd get either of them. We'll have to see how it goes ... Yes. Fancy! Goodbye ... (*He hangs up the telephone*) Sorry, dear. Just future plans. Johnnie, I won't let you run helter-skelter into oblivion. I wouldn't forgive myself.

Gielgud Thank you ——

Binkie The board's meeting at seven to consider ... I'll come straight over afterwards.

Gielgud Oh God! Oh well.

Binkie Please relax. Try to be serene. Behave as you ought in that convenience, dear. Head held high and aloof as a father superior.

Gielgud I suppose I should cultivate a monk's habits from now on.

Binkie What could be more suitable? In public at least. Good luck.

The Lights go down

A soundtrack of voices, chatter as of the rehearsal room. And then a hush

Gielgud is spotlit in the darkness. He faces the audience. He speaks these words (Richard II, 3.3.143-152):

> "What must the king do now? Must he submit?
> The king shall do it. Must he be deposed?
> The king shall be contented. Must he lose
> The name of king? O' God's name let it go. (*He stands*)
> Down, down I come like glistering Phaeton,
> Wanting the manage of unruly jades.
> In the base court? Base court where kings grow base
> To come at traitors' calls and do them grace.
> In the base court? Come down? Down court, down king!
> For night owls shriek, where mounting larks should sing."

Gielgud exits

CURTAIN

ACT II

Scene 1

Gielgud's home. Later the same evening

John Gielgud and Chiltern sit in chairs. Chiltern has a glass of wine, Gielgud smokes, drinks alcohol, walks up and down. He is fraught with anxiety. The atmosphere is sharp with the cloudy airs of anticipation

Gielgud They seem to be taking an ominously long time ——
Chiltern It'll be the lawyers. Frightening Binkie with fantasies — Liverpudlians rioting as soon as you come on.
Gielgud The thought of audiences howling vulgar abuse!
Chiltern I hope Binkie discovers steel under all that plush velvet of his.
Gielgud He's never faced a scandal like me.
Chiltern A pretty small-sized one. An illicit wink. Not a wank.
Gielgud But it's the thought that counts ...
Chiltern Liverpool! What better place to begin a pre-London tour. They're not known for primness. How's your head?
Gielgud Hammering!
Chiltern Aspirins. Take another. May I ask — your mother? Your brother? Did you manage some story?
Gielgud Drunkenness! A policeman mistaking high spirits ...
Chiltern Very dignified.
Gielgud Dignity! I can't wear an air of that any more.
Chiltern Oh, I don't know.
Gielgud I've been far too spoilt and protected.
Chiltern One could say.
Gielgud No wonder Nemesis put me top of her list.
Chiltern Oh Nemesis hasn't got you in her grasp. It's just a nasty dose of hubris.

The bell rings

Gielgud Would you let him in?

Chiltern exits

Gielgud sits; his face falls

Chiltern enters with Binkie in autumnal, gentleman's finery

Gielgud (*standing*) Binkie. (*He extends a hand*)
Binkie John, my dear! (*He holds Gielgud's hand*)
Gielgud A drink?

Binkie nods. Gielgud pours him wine

Binkie Well then! Yes. How are you?
Gielgud Bearing up.

They stand — tense

Binkie We've been talking over the options.
Chiltern Would you like me to leave, John. Or go next door?
Binkie Leaving would be best, Mr Moncrieffe.
Gielgud I'd like him to stay.

A silence

Binkie This is a very personal matter.
Gielgud (*glacially*) Yes. That's why I want Chiltern.
Binkie Mr Moncrieffe. (*He turns to Chiltern*) Well you're — I don't mean to cause offence — you write for a popular newspaper.
Chiltern I'm not some vulgar show business scribbler, Mr Beamount. You're addressing the theatre critic of the *Morning View*. I've no wish to splash my way down to the gutter press level.
Binkie Of course, Mr Moncrieffe. I wouldn't dream of suggesting ——
Gielgud Chiltern stays. What's the decision?
Binkie Decision? We haven't travelled quite that far yet.
Chiltern When do you plan to get there?
Binkie We decided to pause for twenty-four hours. Consider the morning papers and so forth.
Gielgud It'll be ugly ... The audience. I can't bring that on the cast. What did the board say?
Binkie Nothing clear-cut. We're in a wait-and-see position. Can you continue, John?
Chiltern Yes. He must.
Binkie That's not for you to judge ——
Gielgud Binkie — I ought to go and lie down. I didn't sleep at all last night.

Binkie You'll come in just before ten, dear?

Gielgud It depends on the papers.

Binkie And Johnnie — the afternoon run-through — Ralph was quite delighted. Sybil said it went as smoothly as clockwork.

Gielgud Yes, I gave a fairly mechanical performance. Thank you for the cold comfort. Finish your drink. Chiltern will see you out.

Gielgud leaves

There is a silence

Chiltern Dangerous for his future if he withdraws ...

Binkie Oh, my sentiments too, Mr Moncrieffe. But a violent reception. Hisses and boos. Performance stopped. That would be the end. Liverpool. Such a rough town! Sailors and riff-raff.

Chiltern The nauticals are scarcely strangers to gentlemen with gentlemen, Mr Beaumont. Riff-raff won't give a toss. And middle-class theatregoers — they'll be out in force.

Binkie We don't want Mr Hunter's lovely play to miss its West End chance. If they stop buying tickets on the pre-London tour, or if box office advances fall away — well — yes, well!

Chiltern Of course one wouldn't want you to suffer ... some of us worry about John ——

Binkie How lucky for John to find you such a valiant admirer, Mr Moncrieffe.

Chiltern You're generosity itself.

Binkie But if his public desert him — well! Yes! What then?

Chiltern Would you hand him over to the mob because he gazed at a policeman in a public convenience at midnight?

Binkie I'm only thinking of John. He could come back when it's all blown over. In something bright and bijou. A Restoration Comedy perhaps? Congreve's *Love for Love*? Cecil Beaton sets, gorgeous Hardy Amies costumes, Edith and Peggy being witty in elegant dresses.

Chiltern Have you heard what Edith's saying about John?

Binkie No. I never eavesdrop. One risks hearing such disagreeable home truths ...

Chiltern That she gave up the right to walk the streets when they made her a dame and that applies to knights like John as well.

Binkie Yes. I'm afraid dear Edith takes a grim view of the sexual these days, now sex doesn't even give her a first glance. You see, Mr Moncrieffe, imagine the audience stopping the play in Liverpool. Financial disaster. That would finish him.

Chiltern Won't you be sued for thousands if you cancel Liverpool?

Binkie We have the best lawyers. One can always come to terms with a provincial playhouse.

Chiltern Give John your support.

Binkie Oh, yes. Absolutely! I mustn't detain you further.

Chiltern Mr Beaumont, I've something to say ——

Binkie Of course. (*He looks at his watch*) Yes. Do.

Chiltern Your company's made a lot of money out of John. You've not paid him well. He's an innocent about money. You persuaded him he didn't need an agent. Fight for him now.

Binkie He has my support.

Chiltern If he's chucked out in the cold, I warn you — we'll blow the whistle on your whole queer theatre network.

Binkie I see.

Deadly silence; Binkie stares at Chiltern

There's no such network I know of.

Chiltern Are you quite sure?

Binkie You're not exactly in an unexposed position, Mr Moncrieffe. I wouldn't try casting the first stone.

Chiltern I'll take the risk.

Binkie Are you perhaps talking blackmail, Mr Moncrieffe?

Chiltern Stand by him ——

Binkie Well, Mr Moncrieffe. You tread very carefully.

Chiltern If you let the wolves turn on John, Mr Beaumont, you may find they turn on you next.

Binkie walks out

Scene 2

Hampstead Heath, Highgate Hill

A late afternoon of thin, autumnal sunlight. Greg and Terry sit high up on Highgate Hill, close together. An old fashioned Brownie 127 by Terry's side. Greg sits on a copy of the "Evening Standard"

Greg Come on, Terry! Pose ... Just one more. (*He takes hold of the camera*)

Terry (*sitting up*) I'm always posing for you. (*He looks at his watch*) *Pickup On South Street*. It's on at the Gaumont. Six forty.

Greg (*looking at his "Evening Standard"*) It says they've good seats for *Hamlet* left.

Terry Don't be daft. I'm not sitting through Shakespeare, posh boy.

Greg It's Richard Burton. He's a dream-boat. Working class Welshman. You'd fancy him.

Terry Nah! You need some tough boy's cinema. Make a man of you. *Pickup On South Street.*

Greg (*happily*) OK. Make a man of me in the back row of the Gaumont ... But you have to pose first.

Terry I'm not taking me shirt off again, porn boy. Never know who sees your photos.

Greg What a swizz!

Terry (*standing up*) Go on then, flash your little Kodak at me. (*He does a mock-pose of showing his torso*)

Greg Super. Let's stay here a bit more. I want to look at you.

Terry You can have your fill of me. Later. (*He sits down again*)

Greg Wish I could.

Terry Come on. Let's get on the motor.

Greg (*not moving*) I like your bike. It's the one place I can get really close to you in public.

Terry You're a wicked boy, you are. (*He puts a hand round Greg's shoulder*) But I like you.

Greg Thanks.

Terry Hasn't happened before to me like this.

Greg Like what?

Terry Like you.

Greg Bet it has.

Terry (*shaking his head*) Never wanted to be queer.

Greg Nor did I. When did you know?

Terry Last week. Thursday afternoon!

Greg Oh come on.

Terry Couple of years ago.

Greg No! You had girls?

Terry Sure I did. They were keen.

Greg Wow! What happened?

Terry Dunno. It never felt right. I changed!

Greg Thank God.

Terry You wanna see the world with me then?

Greg You mean you'll get out of the Vice?

Terry Dunno? I haven't got a big daddy to find me a decent job.

Greg Of course.

Terry Getting away. It's a dream.

Greg Yes. Yes. But I've got three years of Cambridge. Then bloody National service.

Terry I can see it. You and cockney soldiers! Messing around with Privates' privates.

Greg No. There's only you. Wait for me.

Terry I might.

Greg Where will we go?

Terry We'll follow the sun. We'll do all sorts. I'll buy a boat. Learn to sail. You'll be crew ... We'll dip into Africa. Tangier. On the bike across America. Stop over in Hollywood. And that Montgomery Clift. He'll be filling up his old Buick on Sunset strip. Catch my eye — and want me.

Greg No he won't, you bastard. What will I do? (*He makes to hit Terry*)

Terry (*parrying the blow*) You can watch us — for a bit. You'll like that.

Greg Bastard.

Terry All right I'll leave him — after a night.

Greg Oh, thanks. And after?

Terry We'll hit the road. Find all the best beaches. We'll run for miles. By the shore. Sunset.

Greg Sounds dreamy.

Terry Yeah. It will be.

Greg For always?

Terry Always.

Greg Thanks. Thanks. Terry — I think ——

Terry (*half embarrassed, half delighted*) Yeah I know. Don't say it. Not here.

Greg (*looking around*) I want to.

Terry (*getting up*) It's the wrong time. (*He holds out his arms. He hauls Greg up to stand*)

For a moment Greg and Terry are close. It is Greg's chance

Greg I think I love you.

Terry That's all right. (*He flashes him a smile*) Come on then. You can run after me.

Terry runs off. Greg does too

Queen Mab's, six o'clock

It is the first night of "A Day by the Sea"

The civilized murmur of voices, of hilarity and sotto voce laughter. Brian sings "My Future Just Passed" by Annette Hanshaw as he assembles drinks. Vera is at the bar making some complex cocktail, a task which she accomplishes with weary, athletic nonchalance ... Chiltern is reading the "Evening Standard" at one of the tables. Matthew and Daniel stand at the door to the piano bar, their backs to us

Brian Well Billie Bracknell says they're prepared for a riot in the gallery tonight.

Vera Don't you believe that loose-mouthed queen. Those gallery first-nighters aren't butch enough to riot. They'll just sit there all prissy and pursing their lips when Sir John comes on.

Brian Oh, really, Miss D. When were you last familiar with a gallery first-nighter then?

Chiltern (*putting down his newspaper*) Actually, Vera, I've been told Binkie is having a police presence up there.

Brian See, Vera. A woman in your position just doesn't know the half of it.

Brian departs

Vera (*calling after him*) Position! What would you know about positions, Brian Mandeville, when there's only one you've ever got down to ... (*Addressing herself to Chiltern*) Now dear, a word in your shell-like — while that very young man's out at the shop. Not your usual thing is he?

Chiltern Thing, Vera? You speak as if he's some vulgar knick-knack I acquired for a song in a doubtful antique emporium.

Vera Well. If the dutch cap fits ... I can't help noticing he looks a touch underage. Some sort of nephew I hope. Or second step cousin several times removed.

Chiltern Vera, I assure you, there's nothing to worry about. Gregory's a public school boy ——

Vera That's never a sign of respectability, dear. He's under twenty-one isn't he?

Chiltern What's a year or two when one's young? I scorn petty regulations.

Vera   Gallivanting around with a youngster in tow. I thought you confined yourself to violent guardsmen.

Chiltern   My relationship with Gregory is purely theatrical and flamboyantly platonic. Leave guardsmen out of it.

Vera   I don't think theatrical's very reassuring, dear. And as for that Plato — well, didn't he mess around with youths?

Chiltern   Not for the first time, Vera, your ignorance about Ancient Greece astounds me. You've confused Plato, who rose above queer sex, with Socrates who didn't and enjoyed young men.

Vera   Oh screw Socrates, Chiltern ... Are you aware the police raided the *Pink Monkey* last night?

Chiltern   With a name as camp as that you can hardly blame them.

Vera   The *Pink Monkey*, Chiltern, is an espresso bar. Full of RADA students and innocent shop boys. Well, shop boys anyway. They took down names and addresses. The police are getting so heavy-footed ... Is he of your persuasion this juvenile?

Chiltern   I imagine so. He tells me he's mad about Richard Burton.

Vera   (*delighted*) I hardly think that's a sign. I'm potty about Richard Burton too, but that doesn't make people think I'm a lesbian.

Greg returns with a copy of the "Spectator"

Hello, darling. We were just talking about you.

Greg   (*putting the magazine down on the table and sitting*) Gosh! Why? Here you are, Chiltern. The *New Statesman*'s not in yet.

Chiltern   (*taking the magazine*) Thanks. Gregory, would you please assure Miss Dromgoole that I have no wicked designs upon you.

Greg   Honestly, Vera — if I may call you Vera ——

Vera   You may, darling. And you seem to have managed it very nicely without my permission ——

Greg   Mr Moncrieffe's just giving me the chance of going to a few first nights. We met outside the Old Vic.

Vera   That's very public-spirited, Chiltern. Acting as a theatrical charity for young men, down and out in theatre queues.

Chiltern   I would never go in for teenagers ...

Vera   Yes, but you give the appearance of going out with one. We've got to look respectable.

Chiltern   Respectability. One of the seven deadly virtues. I avoid it at all costs.

Vera   Not in here, darling, you won't. (*To Greg*) Sweetheart, if anyone asks, you're just twenty-one.

Greg   Of course, Vera. Thanks, Vera! It's an age I'd love to be.

Vera   Wouldn't we all, dear! (*She puts two glasses on the table; to Greg*) And don't drink it all at once, dear. It's not Tizer, you know ...

Vera exits with her tray of drinks

Greg What's upset her?

Chiltern She's a bit of a drama queen. Jumping to all the wrong conclusions. (*Pause*) Actually I don't even know your surname.

Greg (*surprised*) Lightbourne.

Chiltern (*disturbed*) Lightbourne! I hope you're no relation of the judge.

Greg Which one?

Chiltern Percival Lightbourne.

Greg No.

Chiltern Ridiculous fellow. Thinks homosexuality's infectious. Says you can be cured if they catch it early enough. He was up at Oxford with me.

Greg We're definitely not related.

Chiltern What a relief!

Greg Did you know him?

Chiltern Very slightly. I played a rather queer Mercutio at the OUDS. He bumped into me the next day. Said what a brave performance I'd given ...

Greg Gosh! Did he fancy you?

Chiltern Oh, he wouldn't have dared! He was all knotted up. Quite a dish though. Come, Greg. Drink up. Let's stroll down to the Haymarket. I need to see there's no trouble as the audience goes in.

Greg You think there will be? After his ovation at Liverpool ...

Chiltern Liverpudlians don't count. Edinburgh gave him the cold shoulder.

Greg It's all so unfair.

Chiltern What is?

Greg The police picking on an innocent man like him.

Chiltern Innocent? Poppycock!

Greg (*defensive and unwise*) How would you know? You weren't there.

Chiltern (*not noticing Greg's indiscretion*) Greg ... He's an addict. A compulsive frequenter of urinals ... Fatal in these witch-hunt times.

Greg (*trying to conceal his devastation*) Oh. I didn't know ...

Chiltern Never mind. The play's the thing. Don't just sit there. Come on.

Greg does not move

Daniel and Matthew standing in the doorway turn and stand facing each other

There is the sound of applause in the piano bar

(*Calling out and standing*) Hallo young men, how are you?
Daniel I guess we're fine.
Chiltern This is Gregory Lightbourne. I found him in a queue for returns. He's my good deed for the month.
Daniel Very generous of you, Chiltern. Hi, Greg! This is Matthew.

Greg stands up; they all shake hands

Greg (*to both*) Well hallo. And goodbye. We're off for *A Day By The Sea.*
Chiltern (*with a theatrical wave*) Gentlemen. Enjoy the pleasures of the night.

Greg and Chiltern go out

Brian's voice is heard from the salon to his own piano accompaniment

Daniel and Matthew stand listening. They keep a fixed gaze on each other

Brian (*off, singing*)
> I was just a seeker after love you know
> I thought of aiming high, but always had a penchant
>   for the low.
> I cruised in cottages and picked up in the usual bars.
> I tried my luck on summer nights in green and open spaces,
> Now ending up alone, of all my loves I'm only left
>   with traces.

Daniel Sad song! I'm sorry.
Matthew Me too.
Daniel You OK?
Matthew Naturally.
Daniel It just doesn't work, does it?
Matthew Oh. Does for me.
Daniel I'm sorry.
Matthew Yes, ah well. I ought to leave.
Daniel Don't go like that.
Matthew There's not anyway else I can.

Matthew and Daniel shake hands

Thanks for it, though.

Daniel It?
Matthew For what was.

Matthew walks out and Daniel follows him

SCENE 4

The Haymarket Theatre

John Gielgud at his dressing-room mirror puts on the finishing touches of make-up. Binkie Beaumont is by his side

There are amplified sounds of an audience out front from the loudspeaker in the dressing-room

Binkie Well, John, dear! It's a fully packed house. Such a distinguished audience. Thrilling atmosphere! I've been eavesdropping out front. Wild anticipation.
Gielgud Yes. I hear the gallery first-nighters are so excited they'll be booing me on.
Binkie We've seen to them. Don't worry. Everyone's friendly — though one can't speak for the critics.
Gielgud Of course, who would want to?
Binkie Though Chiltern will do you proud. And Mr Tynan — he's very homo friendly even if his taste's far too avant garde.
Gielgud I've never had such nerves.
Binkie I think you'll find the audience surprises you.
Gielgud Hmmm! "Oh dear! I'd forgotten we had all those azaleas. When was I last here in May?" At least I won't have to worry about getting a laugh on my entrance.
Binkie Your entrance will tingle with drama.
Gielgud I like the sound of that. Ah well. The readiness is all ... Whatever happens tonight, thank you for fighting my corner.
Binkie Best of luck, Johnnie. My heart goes with you and it's not in my mouth.

The Lights dim. Spotlight on Binkie

Sounds of audience fade

Binkie exits

Gielgud looks at himself in the mirror

Gielgud (*applying extra touches of make-up*) What's happened to my
heart? Beating too fast. Just a little touch of nerves. Could be worse.
Could be doing the Scottish play in the war again. Such an ordeal!
Forced to play butch. Quite beyond me. And Edith refusing to play
my wife. "I could never play a woman who had such peculiar notions
of hospitality." And then two witches dropping dead in rehearsal? So
inconvenient! Duncan collapsing. Dead with angina. Such bad luck ...
Buzz bombers. Cruise overhead ... Engines cut out. Silence. Wait for
the explosion. At least we weren't bombed. What an awful headline.
Gielgud missing in West End hit.
Voice (*off*) One minute, please, Sir John.

Gielgud stands up; he is shaking

Spotlight on Gielgud. He walks

Sybil (*off*) "Julian! If only I could have persuaded him to marry. I'm
sure it would have given him more balance. Some young, cheerful
person! The difference it would have made to him!" (*Calling*) "Julian,
dear! Eighteen years the old man's been here. When he first came he
was wonderfully active, but now — of course. Julian, do come out!"
(*Pause*) "I'll just have to go and bring him into the garden." (*Silence*)

*Sybil appears. She discerns the situation at once and rushes over to
Gielgud*

(*Taking his hand and dragging him forward*) Come on, John darling.
Gielgud My heart's beating wildly. I can't stop trembling
Sybil (*whispering*) It only takes a bit of courage. Your heart will be all
right. Come on.
Gielgud You think so?
Sybil I'm sure, darling. Take my hand. They'll never dare boo me.
Gielgud Hand in hand. At my age! Oh, Sybil!

Gielgud walks out with Sybil and faces the real audience

*We hear a cry or two of "bravo" and a great, enduring outburst of
applause. Applause resounds, more cries of "bravo", then fades*

(*Exultantly*) "I'd forgotten we had all those azaleas. When was I last
here in May?"

SCENE 5

The Home Office, Whitehall. Twilight

Fyfe stands at a lectern by the side of his desk. On the other side of the stage Greg and Terry lie on the floor with bottles of beer. Neither of them wears shoes. They are down to jeans and shirts

The light extends to Greg and Terry for a moment, then falls dark on them

Fyfe "Ladies and Gentlemen of the Tunbridge Wells Conservative Association."

Matthew enters, carrying a doll and some papers

Ah, Mr Barnsbury? What on earth are you doing with that doll?

Matthew I'm sorry.

Fyfe Not at all … I was going to say — they tell me you're leaving the service.

Matthew Yes. I was going to talk to you.

Fyfe I don't understand. You're the best private secretary I've had. A fine future awaits you. What's the problem?

Matthew Thank you. I'm afraid I can't discuss it.

Fyfe I see. Nothing to do with the Home Office, I hope.

Matthew I'm not suited to the service — as things are now.

Fyfe I had no idea. They tell me you're joining the *Observer* to be a leader writer.

Matthew Yes.

Fyfe I'm surprised. It's a very left-wing newspaper, isn't it?

Matthew (*nodding*) I've the statistics you wanted. And the doll — it's the one the DPP wanted you to see.

Fyfe Of course. Yes. (*He steps to the desk and looks at the doll*) It looks a normal accessory for a little girl.

Matthew There's more to it than meets the naked eye, sir, I'm afraid. If you remove its clothing ——

Fyfe Really, Mr Barnsbury! Do you seriously expect me, the Secretary of State for the Home Department, to remove the dress of a female doll, a doll, moreover, that's the subject of a destruction order?

Matthew My apologies, sir. Would you like me to?

Fyfe In your position it would be entirely appropriate. I'll only glance.

Matthew removes the clothing

There's no need to take everything off. Just expose the —— (*He looks*)
It beggars belief. How terrifying if this got into the wrong hands.

Matthew I'm afraid it already has, sir. It was never intended for little
girls ... (*he puts it down on Fyfe's desk*)

Fyfe I don't want that thing soiling my desk. Put it on the floor. Now,
statistics.

Matthew hands over papers. He and Fyfe scrutinize them

*****

The Lights come up on Terry and Greg

*Skeets Macdonald's "Don't Let the Stars Get in your Eyes" plays. It
fades in and out for the remainder of the scene as the action switches
between the two sides of the stage*

*Terry sits turned towards Greg. In the course of the scene, counterpoint-
ing Fyfe, they will further disrobe and become erotic with each other
[See Production Note]*

Greg What about it then? (*He kisses Terry briefly on the mouth*)

Terry What about what?

Greg You didn't listen. "Don't stand in the moonlight while I'm gone."
It means he's singing to a man.

Terry Why's that then?

Greg Women don't loiter in moonlight unless they're tarts.

Terry What you know about girls, butch boy? (*He puts a hand on
Greg's knee*)

Greg Why don't you take off your shirt?

Terry Why don't you?

Greg What?

Terry Take off my shirt. Do it for me. You like that, don't you?

Greg You know I do. (*He turns, unbuttons Terry's shirt and then removes
it*) You look dreamy tonight ...

Terry What? Only tonight?

*****

Matthew On current forecasts ten thousand men will be tried this year
for indictable homosexual offences.

Fyfe (*scribbling on his sheaf of papers*) Excellent! And how do we
compare with the Socialists?

Matthew They imprisoned less than half that number. You may like to know this. (*He points to more figures*) In cases of attempted buggery between young males, half those found guilty were gaoled last year.
Fyfe That's encouraging.

*****

Terry You're a funny boy, you are. (*He puts an arm round Greg's waist*) What about it?

Greg and Terry begin to kiss while the following dialogue takes place

*****

Matthew (*turning a page*) Scotland Yard's report on the Norway conference on obscene literature. Interpol's discovered a link between sex crimes and reading pornography.
Fyfe (*grim relish*) At last! The Scandinavians took pornography lying down far too long.
Matthew It's forecast that we'll be destroying a hundred and sixty thousand obscene books next year.
Fyfe (*leaning over to look at the papers*) And the Socialists only managed a feeble forty thousand annually. Usual pornography I imagine?
Matthew More serious stuff. Gustave Flaubert's *Madame Bovary*, Balzac, Marquis de Sade, Jean Paul Sartre, Jean Genet.
Fyfe It's always foreigners, isn't it? Usually the French. One does business with them — naturally. But they've wicked imaginations.
Matthew And classics too. Magistrates have seized works by Aristophanes, Ovid and Aristotle.
Fyfe It never ceases to amaze me — such a civilization, such genius, the Greeks — yet all this depravity goes straight back to them ...

*****

Terry What you see is what you'll get ...
Greg (*running his hand over Terry's stomach, gazing at him*) I could go on looking for ever. I keep dreaming about you.
Terry Yeah. I been in quite a few X-rated dreams.
Greg I bet you have. (*He runs his hand up and down Terry's biceps*)
Terry You're different, you are. (*He kisses Greg's chest*) What's wrong? You're trembling.
Greg (*looking at him again*) It makes me nervous. Whose home is this?

A pause, but no interruption to the sexual momentum

Terry What's it matter?
Greg You're sure no one's going to come in? (*He does not move*)
Terry Sure I'm sure. My friend's away — d'you do much of this?
Greg What? Which?
Terry Trembling!
Greg Never. Weird isn't it? I blame you.
Terry What you frightened of?
Greg I don't know. (*He takes off his shirt*) You, I think. You make
me —
Terry Make you what? (*Kissing him*) I won't hurt you. You're my guy.

*****

Matthew There've been authorized police swoops on sixteen seaside
shops in Cleethorpes, Bournemouth, Margate, Poole and Swanage
too.
Fyfe I know Cleethorpes. It shows how far depravity's spread, if
Cleethorpes succumbed.
Matthew A picture postcard by Donald McGill. Destruction order on
it... Caption, "The further you're in, the nicer it feels."
Fyfe They printed that on a seaside postcard? Sex, sex, sex, Mr
Barnsbury. England's taking an unnatural interest in it these days ...

*****

Greg (*kissing*) This is really very nice.
Terry Thought you'd like it. Once you got used to the feeling.

*****

Fyfe Just imagine a normal, summer holiday scene. An innocent
fourteen-year-old girl wanders into a Cleethorpes seaside shop. There
she is in her tasteful bathing suit, sucking her Lyons Maid ice-lolly,
singing *How Much Is That Doggy In The Window?* Her little brother
scampers in with his bucket and spade, laughing. She chooses a
postcard of some charming rural scene for her widowed grandmother
in Tunbridge Wells and wham! She can't miss it. "The further you're
in, the nicer it feels." That girl's besmirched. Her childhood innocence
rudely shattered! You don't have to look very far to see what's wrong
with England.

*****

Greg and Terry kiss again, this time more intimately but briefly

Greg I want it to go on for ever.
Terry Kissing?
Greg Yes. More.
Terry Well then, posh boy.
Greg I want you to hold me for always ——
Terry (*holding Greg*) All right?
Greg Amazing — it's like time's stopped. There's only us ...
Terry Go on then. You can have me.

They will gradually shed their clothes and then stand there almost naked, entwined, kissing. Their actions run in counterpoint to Fyfe's speech

*****

Matthew watches Fyfe do his speech

Fyfe   Ladies and Gentlemen of Tunbridge Wells Conservative Association. Something has gone wrong with England, hasn't it? We, the decent majority, upholders of traditional family life, whether in the city or in the heart of the countryside, know it in our hearts. We feel it in our bones ...

*****

Terry I really go for you.

*****

Fyfe The threat of Russia's Cold War, the testing of their H-bombs casts a cloud over us and all the world. Britain faces up to a violent, post-war world where nothing feels certain or safe. Too many people no longer respect the good, old values. The crime rate soars. The would-be murderer with his gun, the violent robber, the teddy boy with his flick-knife menaces us. We look to our judges for security: capital punishment and long prison sentences promise to act as a deterrent. But now we realize some new menace is upon us. We can't see it, we don't hear it, we can't touch it, but we know it's in the air.

*****

Greg There's only us.
Terry Yes.
Greg Love me.
Terry Yeah. Any way you want.

*****

Fyfe Yes, ladies and gentlemen. You and I know there's an infectious plague over England. (*He turns to Matthew*) There you are. As you're leaving us, perhaps I can ask you for your personal view on my speech —
Matthew Of course, Home Secretary. I think it'll go down very well in Tunbridge Wells. You're a perfect match for Senator McCarthy ...

Matthew walks out

Fyfe Mr Barnsbury. Come back. This instance.

Fyfe exits in pursuit of Matthew

*****

Greg I fucking love you.

Terry carries Greg out

SCENE 6

Sybil Thorndike's dressing-room

Sybil is sitting in a chair, removing greasepaint. She studies herself in a mirror. There is a wardrobe, another chair and a plate of two bath buns

Gielgud knocks on the door

Gielgud (*off*) May I trouble you a moment, Sybil?
Sybil (*calling*) Johnnie! Come in.

Gielgud enters

I'm only titivating. Sit down. (*She waves him to a chair*)

Gielgud Sorry to interrupt.

Sybil Would you care for a bath bun?

Gielgud Thank you, Sybil. But they look a bit formidable for me.

Sybil I'm just surveying the old, peeled wall my face has become and giving it a bit of first-aid.

Gielgud Hardly peeled, Sybil. It looks very well fortified...

Sybil Oh John. Always the flatterer! There's a hideous sherry in the wardrobe. Ignore it. That's for visiting enemies. There's a half of champagne. Do open it for us. (*Pause*) No play problems?

Gielgud (*getting out the champagne*) Not at all! We're still a hit. Country house melancholia is all the rage again.

Sybil What did I tell you!

Gielgud Was that Malcolm Sargent I saw flash past me in the corridor? (*He opens the champagne and pours two glasses, then sits down*)

Sybil (*turning round*) Oh Sir Malcolm — yes, rushing off in pursuit of the latest princess or some rendezvous with a duchess.

Gielgud I'm sure he cut me.

Sybil (*turning round, flustered*) No, no dear. He's as blind as a bat. Too vain to wear specs.

Gielgud I'm avoiding people so much, I don't realize they're avoiding me too. I should be glad I've been snubbed by such a top person.

Sybil I dare say there'll be more.

Gielgud What a battered old thing my reputation's become! Battered but not quite bowed.

Sybil You can rise above a dozen Malcolm Sargents.

Gielgud Yes, I try to. Every day. The newspapers just won't leave it alone. The letters. Features. Supplements. It's too much.

Sybil I'm afraid it's your fame, darling. You've brought the problem out into the open.

Gielgud I —— (*a sudden, startling change, a great cry, he weeps, not hiding the tears*) How can I escape myself? How can I be free of it, the whole damned business?

Sybil John! (*She holds his hand*)

Gielgud composes himself. He wipes his face, gathers himself together

Gielgud I'm sorry. I don't know how that happened. I apologize.

Sybil Johnnie. It's all right.

Gielgud Be honest! Malcolm wouldn't see me, would he?

Sybil Poor Malcolm. He doesn't know what a preposterous figure he cuts. Fame does awful things to people. I asked him to say hallo to you. He looked embarrassed, "Oh I couldn't possibly shake hands with him," he said. "You see I mix socially with royalty."

Gielgud Ah! I suppose if he touched my hand, he'd be sexually infected. It might even rub off on some member of the royal family!

Sybil Isn't he romancing the Duchess of Kent?

Gielgud Probably. I like the thought of him rising to conquer.

Sybil Charity. It's a hard life being a queen, but forever chasing a second-tier princess can't be much fun either. It may turn out for the best.

Gielgud For Malcolm or the Duchess?

Sybil For people like you.

Gielgud That'll be the day. (*He pours out the champagne*)

Sybil Here's to it, then. A toast — to a new liberal spirit.

Gielgud and Sybil raise their glasses

Gielgud (*lighter*) Liberal spirit. Is there enough of it around?

SCENE 7

The library of the Polynaeum Club

Greg — in a suit — sits reading the "Evening Standard". He has a cup of coffee by him. No one else is there

Mr Justice Lightbourne enters, dressed in a suit of suitable judicial discretion

Lightbourne sits down opposite Greg

Lightbourne Greg!

Greg (*not looking up*) Yeah? Wait a moment.

Lightbourne It's not as though we often spend time ——

Greg Please. I'm not ready. (*He looks up*) A Day by the Sea. A rave review in *Plays and Players* ... John Gielgud. Remember him? (*He puts down the paper*)

Lightbourne Yes. I glanced at the notices. Let's not discuss his unfortunate behaviour.

Greg Why not? We could chat about loitering coppers. How they tempt men to break the law.

Lightbourne I don't approve of what the police do in lavatories, but that doesn't mean I condone Gielgud's escapade ——

Witherby comes in with port for Lightbourne, a glass of wine for Greg and pot of coffee

Witherby and Greg silently recognize each other

Thank you, Douglas. You found something to my son's taste.
Witherby Your son's got such a sophisticated palate, Sir Percy.
Lightbourne I can't think where he gets it from.
Greg Thanks, Douglas.
Witherby It's a pleasure to meet you at last, Mr Lightbourne.

Witherby exits

Lightbourne What a pathetic old thing he is! (*Pouring out his port*)

Greg takes his wine

(*Pause. Trying to be placatory*) Now, I hope you won't mind. There's
something I want to discuss with you.
Greg (*stonily*) Go on!
Lightbourne I only mention it because you were seen at the theatre the
other day.
Greg Really! What was I supposed to have been doing? Causing gross
offence in the upper circle?
Lightbourne   I   understand   you   were   accompanying   Chiltern
Moncrieffe.
Greg Yes. I was queuing for a first night return. He offered me his
second seat.
Lightbourne Just like that? He hasn't changed. You realize Chiltern
Moncrieffe's a practising — practising —— (*he cannot bring himself
to use the word*)
Greg Practising what? Surely he's got the hang of it by his age?
Lightbourne Don't make me say the word. I have to use it quite
enough.
Greg You won't catch anything by saying it. (*Pause*) Well, he's not
practising on me.
Lightbourne Greg, this is serious. Moncrieffe was up at Oxford in my
time. He was notorious.
Greg For what?
Lightbourne You know perfectly well.
Greg No, you're far more familiar with him than I am.
Lightbourne You know how risky this sort of association is for a young
man.
Greg He's only a practising theatre critic. They're not a danger to
audiences ...
Lightbourne Did you tell him who you were?

Greg In relation to you? Of course not. I'm sorry — you're no boasting matter.

Lightbourne (*pained*) Did he make any ... (*he hesitates*) ... any approach ——

Greg Oh, yes. (*Pause*) An adult approach. He engaged me in conversation ——

Lightbourne May I ask about what?

Greg Theatre.

Lightbourne You seem very preoccupied by the stage.

Greg So?

Lightbourne I hope you're not thinking of a theatrical career.

Greg I may be.

Lightbourne You're such a fine, natural cricketer.

Greg I'm not spending my life with a cricket bat and those stiff upper-class wankers.

Lightbourne You know how common those proclivities are in the theatrical profession.

Greg I don't share your attitudes. It's not an illness. It shouldn't be a crime or a sin.

There is a silence for a moment. Lightbourne and Greg stare at each other

Lightbourne It's a ghastly affliction. Once you succumb — hard to give up, a battle to cure.

Greg Cure! Don't start quoting your Old Bailey judgement at me.

Lightbourne I don't know where you've picked up these radical views. Surely not at school?

Greg We're encouraged to think for ourselves.

Lightbourne How long has this been going on?

Greg Thinking? Oh quite a while, Dad. The young feel free to do it more and more. It's catching on. And judges like you can't do a fucking thing about it.

Lightbourne (*quiet*) Your brother was never like this.

Greg Well, I'm very different.

Lightbourne Where did I go wrong? We tried our best. I didn't let you board at school. I know the dangers when adolescent boys are confined ——

Greg (*in a moment of sympathy*) I'm sorry. Just let me be myself ...

Lightbourne You're at a vulnerable age — and now you're going off the rails ——

Greg You make me sound like some wild train driver hijacking the Perverts' Express.

Lightbourne If you'd heard what I heard in court. I speak from bitter experience.

Greg Well perhaps it's taught you the wrong thing.

Lightbourne It's a terrible life. Desperate. Lonely. Dangerous. You end up with nothing and no one.

Greg What would you know anyway?

Lightbourne The beastly things they do? The infections, the diseases.

Greg (*in anger — he has hit home*) Don't you try and scare me.

Lightbourne (*quietly*) I have to warn you.

Greg Well your duty's done.

Lightbourne And now there's the chance of therapy, of cures.

Greg (*interrupting, with contempt*) They don't want electric shocks and drugs. They don't want therapy, Dad. They just want to be left alone. They won't harm you. Couldn't you leave them alone?

Lightbourne Greg, when one's a young man and easily flattered ——

Greg I'm not listening to this.

Lightbourne To fall like Lucifer — how easy it is!

Greg You picked yourself up OK from whatever depraved position you tumbled into. (*He stands up*)

Lightbourne Where are you going?

Greg Not in the direction you want. I promise you that. (*He walks to the door*)

Lightbourne Please listen ——

Greg opens the door

Greg One thing's clear anyway, Dad. You can go your way. But I'm going mine.

Greg walks out

Lightbourne sits, devastated

Scene 8

Sybil's dressing-room

On the table is a silver coffee jug, milk and biscuits, a script and two sandwiches. Gielgud wears a black patch over his eye. Sybil pours out coffee

Gielgud Perhaps it'll give the play a touch of mystique. Is there something of the pirate about me?

Sybil Not really, dear. Even with that eye patch. Can you see to put in milk?

Gielgud (*nodding*) It comes off next week. But I won't ever look the world in its accusing eye.

Sybil Spam sandwich, dear? Or pilchard?

Gielgud Thank you. But a little too bold for me. Such a relief the doctors let me come back. I've never been off for two weeks before. So dull at home. Hard to read. The dark night of the soul ran and ran.

Sybil Have you stopped seeing double altogether?

Gielgud Just about. The patch gets irritating. I sometimes felt I could scream.

Sybil Nothing to beat a good howl. I was so happy playing Medea.

Gielgud You were always such an enthusiastic howler. They said it was stress, nervous strain. Do eyes have nerves?

Sybil I wouldn't know, dear. (*A little hesitant*) Body parts — I've never taken that much interest.

Gielgud What a refreshing attitude!

Sybil I'm Victorian after all. I mean I thought Lewis shockingly forward when he first held my hand — we'd been walking out for eight months.

Gielgud How quaint it all was then.

Sybil "Would you marry me, Miss Thorndike," he asked. I was shocked.

Gielgud It sounds straight out of Jane Austen.

Sybil (*shaking her head*) I'd much sooner have been a man, Johnnie. It's a bit of a bore being a woman, you know.

Gielgud (*amazed*) I can't say I did. You were always hot for women's rights.

Sybil I mean the erotic side. Thrilling at first I found, but it soon got tiresome.

Gielgud (*embarrassed*) I'm sure you carried on nobly.

Sybil Not often, I'm afraid. I was a bit of a let down on the erotic front. How are you?

Gielgud Even taking a stroll, I half expect jeers or being spat at.

Sybil Spitting's not the done thing. Not in Westminster. And if you go down in the East End — where I hope you don't venture, they wouldn't know you from Dirk Bogarde.

Gielgud A little effeminate isn't he?

Sybil But wildly popular.

Gielgud I actually thought about killing myself — for a few hours after the arrest.

Sybil And a very naughty suicide that would have been.

Gielgud (*taking off his eyepatch*) I'm allowed to take it off a bit. I never thanked you properly.

Sybil For what?
Gielgud You helped stop my ship going down.
Sybil I wasn't going to let you be capsized.

Fred, the doorman, knocks at the door

Come in.

Fred enters

What is it, Fred?
Fred Sorry to disturb, Dame Sybil. (*To Gielgud*) A good luck card for your return, they said, Sir John.
Gielgud Thanks, Fred.

Fred exits

Sybil (*quickly*) John, let me. Don't strain your eyes ...
Gielgud No, no. It's good practice. (*He opens the letter — a card with a newspaper cutting inside. Reading*) "Gielgud ... Hand back your knighthood and repent. The wrath of God is upon you." Ah, a well-wisher! And a newspaper cutting. (*Reading*) "It is often pleaded on behalf of these human dregs they are artistic or intellectual creatures ... we must get such people made moral lepers ... It is utterly wrong men who corrupt and befoul other men should strut in the public eye enjoying adulation and applause ... nation ... mark its abhorence ... stripping from men involved ... any honours ..." *Sunday Express*. (*Shocked*) Have there been many like these?
Sybil A few of them. Enraged Christians. I know how to deal with them.
Gielgud Religion seems to bring out cruelty in people.
Sybil Well not always. I keep my faith.
Gielgud Of course. I stopped reading the papers. I didn't realize.
Sybil Better you didn't. John — I wish something ——
Gielgud What?
Sybil That you'd stop punishing yourself.
Gielgud It's not that easy. I've been a distress and trouble to you all.
Sybil Not at all, darling. You've just been a bit of a silly bugger. And an unlucky one.

SCENE 9

Summer 1956

A back projection of trees. There are two chairs on stage

Terry sits in one of the chairs listening to Elvis Presley on a radio or EP player

Greg appears. He wears a knapsack

Greg Sorry. Sorry. Am I late?

Terry Only two hours. Don't worry. Be as late as you like.

Greg What do you mean? It was the first Hugo Betti rehearsal. I waited for a lift to come down.

Terry Hugo Betty. Betty Hugo. Doesn't matter.

Greg What are you being like this for? (*He turns off the radio and kisses Terry*)

Terry D'you mind — I was listening.

Greg Presley can wait.

Terry Yeah — and I can wait for you. Sorry, but no thanks.

Greg What are you on about? Why you being so sulky? Aren't I allowed to have a bit of fun acting?

Terry Have as much fun as you like. You can find yourself a posh young man up there too. I don't care.

Greg Oh come on. This is silly.

Terry I'm sorry, but I'm not going on with it.

Greg What? (*He sits down*)

Terry It just don't work any more.

Greg Why?

Terry You've got your new life up there. It's all different now. You don't need me.

Greg I don't believe this.

Terry You were ashamed of me when I came to see your play.

Greg I wasn't. I wasn't. Honestly!

Terry You don't ever ask me up there now.

Greg It's just you don't fit in easily.

Terry You're all the same. You middle-class queer boys. I don't know why I keep getting mixed up with your sort. You just want a bit of the rough stuff on the side.

Greg D'you have to play the working man who's hard done by?

Terry Don't you fucking start on class. I haven't got what you've got. Shame. You're just a fucked up university boy, guilty about having a policeman for sex. Oh Nigel, have you met Terry? Actually he's a policeman. Wow, really? Fancy that, Terry. Is it interesting? It must be exciting on Saturday night. Load of fucking poofs!

Greg I'm sorry. You make my life ...

Terry Don't talk stuff. You'll get a degree. Be given a good job by one of Daddy's friends. There'll be lots of posh wankers to play around with. Nigel and Rupert and Tristan and Dominic. All of you picking up sailors and scaffolders and soldiers.

Greg Have you got someone else?

Terry Not yet. But I've had offers.

Greg Who?

Terry Don't worry. No one middle class. I know my place. I've learnt my lesson.

Greg Please — give me one more chance.

Terry You're even ashamed to let me meet your parents.

Greg I couldn't. They'd be ——

Terry Of course. Your father'd have a stroke — and your mother hysterics.

Greg (*after a pause*) I can't bear it. Without you. I can't go back to life without you. (*He is on the verge of tears*)

Terry Greg. (*He puts an arm round him*)

Greg I don't want anyone. I want you. You make me feel safe. I lost my fear with you. Please! Please!

Terry Sorry.

Greg (*in tears*) You made my life work. Don't you see? Without you. I won't bear it. I promise. I can't.

Terry Don't be like this.

Greg I'll be better. I'll be different. I'll do anything to keep you.

Terry (*shocked by this abjectness*) You've tried to be. You're too superior.

Greg Anything ... I'll change. Just give me one more chance. Please. I'm finished without you.

Terry I'm sorry, really sorry. (*He is poised to go*)

Greg Don't go — one more chance. (*He gets hold of him with the strength of the desperate to stop him leaving*)

Terry fights him off

(*Angrily*) You won't get anyone like me again.

Terry (*enraged*) You stupid, stuck up queen. I don't fucking want anyone like you. (*He hits Greg*)

Greg staggers back, falls shocked. Terry helps him up

You OK?

Greg nods

I'm sorry. I love you. But it won't work, posh boy. (*He kisses him, holds him*)
Greg (*overwhelmed*) Please stay.
Terry I can't. I can't take it any more. It makes me too sad.

Terry walks out at speed

Greg stumbles in the opposite direction, all slow and shocked

SCENE 10

Hyde Park by the Serpentine. February 1975

Music plays, then fades: David Bowie's "Ziggy Stardust"

Gielgud and Chiltern sit at a small table. Gielgud, now 71, has aged well. Dressed impeccably in the style of a Harley Street consultant or a Lord of Appeal, he smokes a Turkish cigarette and drinks coffee. Chiltern, fatter, drunker and sleepier than before enjoys a silver flagon of champagne to which he helps himself generously

Voice (*off*) "The Conservative Party has become the first political party in Britain to elect a woman as its leader. Mrs Margaret Thatcher, the former Education Secretary, has won a landslide victory over the other four male candidates to become the leader of the Conservatives. Mrs Thatcher, who had a sixty-seven majority over the nearest contender, former Northern Ireland contender William Whitelaw, rejected suggestions of celebrations.
Voice of Thatcher Good heavens, no. There's work to be done.
Gielgud I've had a remarkable offer.
Chiltern Oh dear! Be safe. Say no.
Gielgud (*benignly*) It might bring out the best in me.
Chiltern At your age? Most unlikely.
Gielgud They've asked me to play a rather queer character. A Pinter. Do I dare?
Chiltern Oh, it doesn't take courage to play one of us these days. Everyone's doing it! Look at Noël! What was that ghastly gay weepie he wrote — after his unwise facelift.

Gielgud *A Song at Twilight* — more of a queer moan before midnight I thought. Besides, Noël was never caught in a gay sex scandal.

Chiltern It's all out of the closet now, Johnnie ... Even the Royal Shakespeare — the play about the tragic gay hairdresser ...

Gielgud Oh. I'd never play one of those. I couldn't manage the hand gestures.

Chiltern All this Gay Liberation stuff. Proud to be queer! I ask you! Flaunting and flouncing on the streets. It's like waving red condoms at bulls! What more do they want? We're legal in England and Wales. Isn't that enough?

Gielgud (*flippantly*) All done strictly in private by over twenty-ones. No one else in the house. No one even allowed to watch.

Chiltern They can't cater for orgies. Or gay voyeurs like you. Think of the crowds there'd be. Thank God they're closing the public latrines. Taking temptation out of your hands at last.

Gielgud (*thoughtfully*) Those Gay Liberationists — rather brave ... This play. The details — they mustn't appear in your paper's diary.

Chiltern Really, John! I, turn you into a gossip item? Don't you remember? The paper sacked me in January.

Gielgud I thought you fell asleep in the stalls. And snored.

Chiltern I hardly think falling into a small snooze over Beckett's *Endgame* constitutes anything but a sign of instinctive good judgment ...

Gielgud I dare say. But your snoring understandably stole the show.

Chiltern I suppose you're doing *The Collection*. The queer antique dealer. Almost typecasting.

Gielgud I'm a poet — picked up on Hampstead Heath by a millionaire played by Ralph.

Chiltern H'mm. I hope it's not an old queer romance.

Gielgud God, no. It all turns respectably hetero. There's just a wholesome reference to a male member in the female mouth. I thought Ralph would object. "Pure fantasy", he said. "Couldn't happen in real life." Such lovely innocence.

Chiltern Well, have a go! After all, you like splashing around with the new wavers these days.

Gielgud To think that once I was fearful of taking the plunge ——

Chiltern (*emboldened by alcohol*) I'll give you this, though. You came out of that lavatorial drama a greater actor.

Gielgud Oh — that old wives' tale! Humiliation helps you plumb your own lower depths.

Chiltern You became more spontaneous on stage — more natural.

Gielgud What a horrible thought!

Chiltern I make the point. In your obituary. Wrote it only a month ago. Reads rather well.

Gielgud But would this Pinter performance inspire snide articles — mentioning my inferno in fifty-three?

Chiltern That's all forgotten now. You don't know how lucky you are. Being in work at seventy-one. So what's left for me? Theatrical memoirs? "From Pinero to Pinter — a full life in the stalls?" I haven't the stamina. Sex? It's so hard to arrange nowadays. Guardsmen — now they're virtually under lock and key. Can't get one's hands on them for love or money. At least you've had an affair or two … I've had next to nothing.

Gielgud I'm so sorry, Chiltern, I know it's awful to be chucked out in the cold and all those people saying you're frightfully old-fashioned and drunk.

Chiltern (*outraged*) Me? Old-fashioned. I'm the first to applaud the true avant garde.

Gielgud Of course. No. Yes. You always used to have your finger right there — I mean you still do.

Chiltern I wonder, I really wonder, John. You ride high now. But none of us told you then what damage you caused with your midnight madness in Dudmaston Mews.

Gielgud (*shocked*) What d'you mean?

Chiltern I know everyone rallied round and wrote you nice letters. But behind the scenes we were appalled. You encouraged the world to believe we were all prone to trailing around murky pissoirs by night.

Gielgud I didn't encourage anyone.

Chiltern I know what Noël said in his letter to you — but you should have seen his diary — he thought you set our cause back by decades.

Gielgud What would you have me do. Sackcloth and ashes weekly for life. I still have the scars. You'll say I deserve them. All right — I do.

Chiltern pours more champagne

Chiltern (*with infuriating condescension*) I wouldn't go that far.

Gielgud I did, I deserved the whole caboodle.

Chiltern Oh, quite the masochist now.

Pause

Gielgud Not at all. I was arrested six months earlier as well. They caught me in the Vale of Health.

Chiltern Christ Almighty!

Pause

Gielgud I've never told anybody. The station sergeant saved me. He told the young PC I was just rehearsing. For a play. They sent me home. I had my chance. I threw it away.

Chiltern (*shocked*) Oh John.

Gielgud Yes. (*Pause*) I lied to you the night they arrested me.

Chiltern Which lie was that?

Gielgud Saying I went to Dudmaston Mews to pee — I did go to look — in spite of your warning.

Chiltern Yes.

Gielgud You're not surprised.

Chiltern I always thought you were lying. Oh, John. Dudmaston Mews — it was off your route home.

Gielgud I didn't realize you had such an A to Z mind. Did everyone realize?

Chiltern I think so. It wasn't a subject worth discussing.

Gielgud But you never said a word.

Chiltern Of course not. Oh, Johnnie, Johnnie. I shouldn't be saying this. But the second bottle gives me permish — I mean I've known you more than fifty years back. And we got together when we were young ... and it was — it was ——

Gielgud Yes — it was ...

Chiltern All that longing for danger and darkness. Never taking love seriously.

Gielgud What an awful thing to say ... People were always stealing my heart. And running off with it.

Chiltern Well, your body was always up for grabs. The heart was your one organ you kept close to yourself ... Always fluttering off to find some fresh flower — (*lighter*) or fruit.

Gielgud (*hurt*) How can you judge? You're the only man you ever fell for. It's not my fault you never hit it off with yourself.

Chiltern (*insistent*) If you'd lived through your heart, perhaps you'd never have had this disastrous lavatory addiction.

Gielgud What sentimental nonsense!

Chiltern Do you think a man of your age, a freshly minted knight of the realm, should have been conducting his sexual affairs on the floor of a municipal convenience, a public urinal of notorious reputation? Tell me that!

Gielgud Of course not! I've changed. I've been with Martin for years.

Chiltern Yes and has he checked that roving eye of yours?

Gielgud That's rich — coming from a man addicted to guardsmen.

Chiltern They weren't dangerous. They were honourable.

Gielgud Except when they knocked you around and stole your money.

Chiltern That was exceptional. They became friends. Some married. You still carried on with them. And what does Martin do? Forces you to go and live in the country.

A Waiter comes to take away the accumulated crockery

Waiter exits

Chiltern dozes. Gielgud, lost in thought, does not notice

Gielgud I wasn't forced. You play with the cards you're given. Or the only ones you've got left...

Chiltern snores

Oh Chiltern! What's the use of a sleeping critic? I can't even get angry with you. (*Pause; he looks at Chiltern*) Who would imagine you were beautiful once? Isn't it strange — how you stole my heart. (*Pause*) When we were young and my heart was still there for stealing and my hopes were high.

Chiltern snores

SCENE 11

Greg's office

A back projection of trees in Lincoln's Inn Fields

The Lights come up on Greg, now forty years old. Some suggestion that this is a barrister's room. There is a bottle of wine on a side table. Lightbourne, now in his late sixties, spruce, suited, becalmed, stands drinking a glass with Greg

Greg I'm trying to help them frame this gay equality bill.
Lightbourne You might as well plan flying to the moon. Who's them anyway?
Greg The Campaign for Homosexual Equality.
Lightbourne Of course. I don't suppose you'd like a little supper at the Polynaeum?
Greg I'd love to, but I'm going to Queen Mab's. It's an anniversary. John Gielgud's speaking. I've been invited.

Lightbourne Ah. Yes. Gielgud. Very pleasant. How much equality are you striving for?

Greg Making us legal in Scotland and Wales. Age of consent at sixteen.

Lightbourne What a dream! A mountain of prejudice to bring down.

Greg Mountains have to be moved.

Lightbourne The Prime Minister hates the whole subject. People won't stand for it.

Greg Well, we'll have to dissolve the people and form a new electorate…

Lightbourne Be realistic. Try for an age of consent at eighteen. My fellow peers might go for that.

Greg No harm in aiming high.

Lightbourne You know Edmund Davis's Criminal Law Revision Committee?

Greg Unfortunately. Nasty old Welsh bigot.

Lightbourne Certainly Welsh. Home Secretary wants it to look at the age of consent. He's asked if I'd join the committee.

Greg Will you have the courage to go for equality?

Lightbourne I'm afraid not, old boy. I'm a practising realist.

Greg Even that's a pretty big leap for you — all things considered.

Lightbourne You're too generous. I'd go for eighteen. And reform for Scotland and Northern Ireland.

Greg (*looking at him*) It's rather unnatural, isn't it?

Lightbourne What?

Greg You turning out to be liberal — and a Law Lord. What did it, I wonder?

Lightbourne Oh, time — and change — and knowledge.

Greg Who gave you those modern accoutrements, then?

Lightbourne I don't know. I looked around. I took a fresh view (*Pause*) Then there was you.

Greg Oh I've not turned out to be anything much.

Lightbourne I disagree. Commitment. Bravery. Discretion. That's more than something.

Greg There's quite enough missing.

Lightbourne Plenty of time. To fill the gaps. Come on, old boy. (*A gesture*) How Shakespearian. You that way — for Mab's and Gielgud. Me — this way for the Garrick. But we can still walk out together.

Greg Thanks, Dad. Thanks.

Queen Mab's. Spring 1975

An anniversary party to celebrate the 35th birthday of Queen Mab's. There is a murmur of voices, laughter and old music from the salon. The songs begin with Porter's "Let's Fall in Love". Daniel and Greg stand talking at the bar. Greg has taken a drug, the impact of which will make him increasingly euphoric and dreamy. Brian is making up cocktails. Chiltern, made dozy by alcohol, sits at a table

Daniel What are you on?
Greg How did you know? Yes. I'm riding high. Someone gave me a Drinamyl …
Daniel I'm mad about them, man. They're rare. Who gave you ——
Greg Some long-haired old guy in the salon. You're looking fabulous — I was wild about you in fifty-three.
Daniel Yeah, thanks that's nice. You were cute. Still are. (*He puts an arm round Greg*)
Brian (*almost to himself*) I was always a Mandrax girl myself. They're serious fun.
Greg I'm trying to embrace middle age. But I don't like the feel of it. I said goodbye to my youth. I wept to see it go.
Brian You're not that much more than a chicken yourself.
Greg Some chicken! More a capon now.
Daniel Sad we won't accept youth as just a visiting buddy.
Greg Why did you stay here — isn't it more fun to be gay in America now?
Daniel Yes — I was caught in the queer witch hunt. Kicked out the service. I'll never go back.
Greg I didn't know.
Daniel Yeah. The Lavender Panic. They used a polygraph on me.
Greg The things I never knew … Whatever happened to Matthew?
Daniel Found himself a heart specialist — for love ... And you?
Greg No one ... Are you hitched up?
Daniel Unhitched just now — which is why I got a date. Sneaking away before Vera's back. Like to have a dinner, some night? (*He hands Greg a card*)
Greg Thanks. I would. Thanks. Let's chase old times.

Greg takes Daniel's card and shakes his hand

We'll meet. (*He sits down wreathed in the synthetic glow of the Drinamyl's magic*)

Daniel It's a deal. (*Leaving*) See you again Brian, one of these nights. Tell Vera I love her.

Daniel exits

Brian She always fancied him. Poor cow.

Greg (*to Brian*) You certainly don't show your age.

Brian I should think not. It'd be gross indecency if I did. Lady Luck gives me the cold shoulder these days, dear. I'm that arthritic, I couldn't do a high kick, even if someone gave me an offer I wouldn't refuse. It's the legs that go in the end.

Greg Yes. Use your talent while it still works.

Brian I try not to miss a trick these days. Miss D — she'll be coming for me any time ...

Greg You and Vera still squabbling?

Brian No dear — the other Miss D — Death herself ... "*Carpe diem*" Chiltern keeps telling me. I used to think it was some top Italian cocktail.

Greg I don't know if I dare talk to Gielgud. I'm too high.

Brian Oh, go on! I'll whisk you up a double espresso on the rocks. You won't know yourself.

Greg OK. I'll just go and shock my face in cold water. (*He gets up and passes by Chiltern*) Hallo, Chiltern.

Chiltern (*startled, opening his eyes*) Ah yes. How kind of you ... Yes. I reviewed you at the Royal Court I think.

Greg walks out

Vera and Gielgud sweep in

Vera is dressed to the nines, decorated with far too much jewellery and already a victim of too much alcohol. Vera and Gielgud sit down at another table

Vera Now be honest, darling, it's not a bore saying a few words to the Old Queen Mabbers?

Gielgud (*distracted, gazes in alarm at Chiltern*) Yes. Of course it is. You're absolutely right.

Vera Oh, well if you feel like that? Just don't do it.

Gielgud No, no I look at you, darling, and you — you bring back the war for me with an almighty bang.

Vera Well, thanks a bundle.

Gielgud It's the force of your personality. You're like the other Vera — you put nostalgia back into the blitz.

Vera (*half flattered*) I always thought Vera Lynn's voice was a bit whiney myself, and as for those songs! That reminds me, darling — Brian, bring Sir John another cocktail — I thought it'd be lovely if —

Gielgud (*suspicious*) What's in these cocktails exactly?

Vera Brian's bombe surprise from nineteen forty-five! What's in it, Brian?

Brian Brian's Number One Cocktail Mystery. Magic. (*He walks over to Chiltern and fills his glass*)

Gielgud It's not drugged, is it?

Vera Oh the poor thing wouldn't know one drug from another, would you Brian?

Brian Of course. Nothing illegal passes my lips these days, dear.

Chiltern (*drinking*) It's certainly got a rare kick to it.

Gielgud (*aside*) Chiltern. I'm not having you fall asleep again.

Vera (*distracted*) If only we aged beautifully like trees and turned golden and orange and bronze ...

Gielgud You still look pretty golden to me, darling ... So clever your blonde hair with brunette eyebrows. How do you do it?

Vera Oh, Sir John. You don't miss a trick. We've missed you ...

Gielgud Yes, a delight to be here. But everyone seems so flamboyantly old. You said you had exciting young members.

Vera The young — they don't want a chic club like Mabs. Our gay glamour's gone out of fashion ... It's all sex and disco now.

Gielgud (*looking at his watch*) Yes. All very alien to me. Everything exposed or out in the open. Most alarming ... Isn't it time I cut the cake, Vera? You know I can't stay long.

Vera It'll be lovely, Johnnie. I'll say a few words — how you and Chiltern were here just hours before —

Gielgud Oh no, Vera, I wouldn't allow it.

Vera But nobody worries now, dear. Gays are even marching all over the shop ...

Gielgud No, Vera, no. I'm not having my unsavoury past served up with a pink anniversary cake.

Vera Oh well, dear! Please yourself. You and Chiltern stay here. Soon as we start playing *These Foolish Things* they'll all stand up and you'll make your entrance. Brian'll give you your cue. (*She walks past Brian; under her breath*) Ungrateful old poof he is!

Vera exits

Gielgud Chiltern! Pull yourself together! I'm only here because of you. All these pathetic, old members gazing at me as if I were something stuffed in a glass case. So depressing — the way they gamely shuffle around.

Chiltern She'll be mentioning my role in putting Mab's on the gay map.

Greg returns and sits down at a small table away from Chiltern and Gielgud

Gielgud Chiltern — please — stop this aimless drinking.
Chiltern Naturally people here are asking about my memoirs. *First Night Sensations* — did I tell you the title?
Gielgud Have you any cigarettes? I've smoked my last.
Chiltern My doctor's deprived me of all the innocent pleasures.
Gielgud (*alluding to Greg*) That attractive boy over there. He smiled at me.
Chiltern (*peering*) Really, Johnnie! Boy! That's no boy. He's positively middle-aged. An actor, I think.
Gielgud Ah well. He was young when I looked. Time's winged chariot keeps breaking the speed limit these days. Ripeness is all. Or almost.
Chiltern Anyway he smiled at me. Not you.
Gielgud No need to be jealous. We both look like anaemic walnuts now.
Chiltern I like to look on myself as a rather superior fruit.
Gielgud I couldn't have put it better myself. Anyway. It's all quiet in the Y-fronts nowadays, as far I'm concerned.
Chiltern What a relief for us all that is! (*He closes his eyes*) I couldn't face another uprising.

Greg sits enraptured by the waves of Drinamyl that course through him. Gielgud moves over to him

Brian draws down the shutters on the bar and leaves

Gielgud I hope you won't mind my asking, but I've run out of cigarettes.
Greg (*rubbing his eyes, startled, amazed, standing*) Sure! Somewhere. (*He produces a packet and lights one for Gielgud*) Take the rest! I don't need them tonight.

A dream-like alteration of scene begins to take place

Witherby appears in his brown overall and begins to remove the furniture from Queen Mab's. Scene changers will help him to clear the place

The Lights flicker and begin to fade and turn to silvery mistiness

Gielgud That's extraordinarily generous of you.
Greg Well, I'm under a better influence than nicotine. (*He stands up, looks around in confusion*) What's happening?
Gielgud Have we met before? Acted together? There's something a bit *déjà vu* about you.
Greg Where's Brian gone? I ——

Gielgud smiles and says nothing

I'm no actor. We did meet. I'm sorry, I was blissed out. Now you turn up.

The sound of "These Foolish Things" begins to play

Brian reappears and goes over to Chiltern, takes his arm and leads him out

Vera (*off; sounding like an echo in a large empty space; her voice beginning to fade as the speech goes on*) Hallo Queen Mabbers and welcome to our thirty-fifth anniversary which — I'm afraid — is our last big night. I'm sad to say the carnival's over. Mab's has two months left in this building. The lease runs out. They're knocking this old house down to develop it.

There are sounds of dismay

Yes! I'm afraid we can't reopen. It's a tragedy! But first, to look back and cut the cake, who better than our own and very lovely Sir John Gielgud? He's here to send us on our way and into history. (*Repeating the words as if a record was caught in repetition*) Sir John. Sir John. Sir John.

Gielgud does not react. It's as though he can't hear Vera

Greg I know. It's time for us to go back together.
Gielgud Where are you taking me?
Greg Will you follow me?
Gielgud Is it safe?
Greg We'll only know when we get there.
Gielgud I'll chance it then. I rarely resist being led astray by a promising young man.

Greg You don't have to tell me.

The lighting turns blue. Brian Eno's "Music for Airports" plays. The murmur of voices and Vera's voice fade away into nothingness

SCENE 13

Dudmaston Mews public lavatory

"Music for Airports" continues to play

The stage is physically transformed. The cocktail cabinet revolves to disclose the outlines of the lavatory urinals, but only in fragmented, dilapidated outline. All the doors of the cubicles swing open as if on broken hinges — except for one. Greg and Gielgud walk in a slow circle and end up standing by the wash basin. From Witherby's cubicle comes the sound of Evelyn Laye singing "I'll See You Again"

Gielgud (*looking round*) All this looks disquietingly familiar.
Greg So it should. We're back.
Gielgud Is this not one of London's most infamous public conveniences?
Greg It's what we have in common.
Gielgud I hope no part of me ventured impertinently in your direction.
Greg I wasn't your target.
Gielgud "I'll see you again!" Hardly the sort of sentiment to be expressed in a urinal, is it? Even with Evelyn Laye singing.
Greg How frighteningly romantic.
Gielgud (*shocked*) What folly to look for romance in here. It turns up at stage doors. Not latrines.
Greg This is where it was for me.
Gielgud I don't even know your name.
Greg Greg! (*He holds out a hand*) We meet again!

Witherby comes towards them with a pail of water, cloths and dusters

Gielgud Again! Well, if you say so.

Gielgud and Greg shake hands

Witherby Evening, gents. Trip down memory lane before we close down? (*He puts down the pail and begins to clean the basins*)
Greg Well I'm sort of tripping.

Witherby It's vandalism, isn't it? Closing a precious antique WC like this.

Gielgud I've very mixed memories.

Witherby (*pausing from cleaning*) I'm afraid we got too popular.

Greg This place changed my life.

Witherby Well isn't that nice, sir. People love the place. The letters of thanks I've had. Thirteen in all.

Greg It's haunted here.

Witherby Oh yes. We're no strangers to gay apparitions.

Gielgud Sex rears its head in such risky places. An ever-dangling sword of Damocles.

Greg Sometimes even love.

Witherby Damocles — yes! You wouldn't believe it, but I'm sixty-three and a quarter. I couldn't take on another convenience now. After Dudmaston Mews it would be such a big come-down. (*He moves towards one of the lavatory cubicles, whose door is half open; gasps*) Oh my goodness, it's happened again.

Greg (*with interest, moving over*) What has?

Witherby Don't look, sir. (*To Greg*) The old gentleman — he'll only be shocked!

Gielgud (*approaching, in curiosity*) Don't worry. I've been exposed to the rougher side of life.

Witherby "There are fairies at the bottoms of my guardsmen." I don't know about that ...

Gielgud People will fantasize.

Witherby I'm sorry, sir. I take this seriously. I need my Chemico.

Witherby bustles away

Greg That night ——

Gielgud When?

Greg — they arrested you.

Gielgud No. You're too young.

Greg I was almost nineteen. Remember me?

Gielgud No. I can't.

Greg (*angrily*) Go on. Stop pretending. You've known all along. (*Pause*)

Gielgud Yes. I realized it was you.

Greg Who's me?

Gielgud You're the young man. In here. That night.

Greg What did I do?

Gielgud You tried to save me.

Greg Yes. I couldn't persuade the policeman.

Gielgud What a fatal dish to set before a queen!

Greg But why were you here — and often?

Gielgud I was always tempted by risk – and danger.

Greg I was just looking.

Gielgud An attractive boy of eighteen. In here. Why?

Greg walks to the wash basin. He stands there

Greg I'm eighteen again. No one in the world knows I'm gay. I'm anxious all the time.

Gielgud Yes.

Greg I'm only here to watch.

Gielgud All those rushed anonymous climaxes.

Greg Best just to fantasize.

Gielgud Ah. Yes.

Greg This young man. He won't give me a glance. Madness — I follow him out. He stands talking to a man in a car. I go back in. Then you walk in. I know you. I watched you three times in *Venice Preserv'd* that summer.

Gielgud "My Lord, my Lord. I'm not that abject wretch you think me." But that night I had no intentions ——

Greg Yes. As you leave — he comes back, gives you that look. And I get this hunch he's police.

Pause

Gielgud But you don't walk away.

Greg I'm mesmerized. I want to watch.

Gielgud Yes.

Greg I didn't even know you were queer. I wanted to save you. I betrayed you instead.

Gielgud There's nothing to say.

Silence. Then the song "Don't Let The Stars Get In Your Eyes" begins. The only closed cubicle door begins to open. Greg and Gielgud are shocked

Greg There's someone in there.

Terry nonchalantly appears through the cubicle door. True to Greg's hallucination. He has not aged at all. He is still in his early to mid twenties

Terry 'Allo there. You back for the big finale too?

Greg (*shocked, transfixed*) Terry!

*Faintly outside, the sound of chanting Gay Liberation marchers —
first heard as cries and cheers and whistles increasing in volume and
vehemence as the procession approaches and then begins to fade away*

(*To Gielgud*) You know who this is?

Gielgud How could I forget!

Terry Stone the nancy boys — it's Greg. (*He listens*) They're playing
our song.

Greg But why are you still so young? You look not a day over
twenty-five.

Terry Here's looking at you again.

Greg and Terry shake hands. They embrace — close and long

I've given time the run-round, haven't I.

Greg You remember him? (*He nods towards Gielgud*)

Terry Your face rings a bell. But I can't put a name to it. Sorry.

Gielgud Don't reproach yourself.

*The sounds of marchers begins: "Give us a G, give us an A, give us a
Y — GAY."*

Terry Wait a minute. Didn't I arrest you once?

Gielgud You did indeed. Fortunately there wasn't a twice.

Terry Sorry about that. It's no excuse, my boss got me on to you. Said
you was a regular. "You'll get a rise out of him."

Gielgud And you did of course.

Terry But I gave up the force in the end. Greg was always going on at
me ——

Gielgud (*turning to Greg*) Am I to deduce, Greg, you managed to pick
up this policeman from the wreckage of my career as a cruiser?

Greg That too.

Gielgud At least I was the lightning rod for someone's pleasure that
night.

Terry Well I'll be buggered in the catacombs. I know you. Weren't you
Frankenstein on the box? Weren't you John Gielgud?

Gielgud Yes I was. Still am.

Terry I don't suppose you'd shake hands?

Gielgud (*after a pause*) Certainly. No hard feelings now. (*He extends
his hand*)

Terry shakes Gielgud's hand

Who would have thought I'd end up shaking anything of yours? You winked at me.

Terry Yeah, but you smiled back.

Witherby walks briskly down to them

Witherby Well, gents. You won't believe this. But there're these queer marchers coming down our way. And people coming out to look.

There are now regular cries of "Give us a G, give us an A, give us a Y – GAY!"

Greg In this street!

Witherby Oh yes! Hundreds ... And what they're wearing! I don't know how they dare!

Gielgud How fascinating. I'd love to gaze ...

Witherby You come with me, sir. I'll bring you out a chair. You can have a ring-side look.

Gielgud Oh no. I have to be discreet. (*To Terry and Greg*) I've never seen queer marchers in the flesh.

Greg You'll find they look fairly human.

Witherby escorts Gielgud out

Terry and Greg stand looking at each other. The chanting of the marchers intensifies through their scene

New music: Scott Walker's "No Regrets"

Greg turns away, overwhelmed by emotion

Terry What's the matter?

Terry turns Greg round so they face each other

Greg — Greg, posh boy.

Greg Have you come back for me?

Terry I can't come back.

Chant of "We're here. We're queer. You'd better get used to it."

Greg I suppose I knew.

Terry You on the drugs? Up to no good with stuff?

Greg Purple hearts. Mandrax. Dexedrine. Quaaludes, cocaine. Drinamyl.
I loved them all. But you made me blissed out best.

Terry That's nice. You still got all the photos we took of us.

Greg I can't look at them any more.

Terry Got yourself mixed up with another muscle boy, did you?

Greg No. What about you?

Terry I been and done the world.

Greg (*upset*) We were going to go together.

More chants: "We're here. We're not going away."

Terry It would have been good.

More chanting: "We're here, we're queer. You'd better get used to it."

Greg (*rapt*) On your motor bike?

Terry Yeah ... All the hot summers. All down Europe.

Greg Did you learn to sail? Did you have lovers?

Terry I got crazy about sailing. Love? There was a bit of that too.

Greg Did you run on all those beaches at sunset?

Terry I ran through summers.

Greg We could have had them together. You had the luck.

Terry Luck! It's you poor little, rich boys who get that on tap.

Greg I searched for you. You've haunted me.

Terry That's nice.

Greg Why did you have to leave me?

Terry The trouble with you, Greg. You was a snob. Ashamed of me
at Cambridge. Afraid to tell your parents you was queer and with a
working man.

Greg I'd be happy to take you to them now.

Terry Too late. Why didn't you fight for me then?

Greg I didn't have the guts.

Silence

Terry I'll hold you for a while — all right?

Greg You're lost to me. You mattered most.

Terry I know. (*He holds Greg*) Sweetheart.

Greg (*astonished*) Magic. I'm nineteen all over again. (*He traces his
hand over Terry's face*) Don't slip away ... Don't go.

*Cries of "We're here, we're queer. We're not going away. You'd better
get used to it."*

Terry Know something? I think I was in love with you.
Greg Yes.

Music fades

 Gielgud and Witherby enter the lavatory. As they walk back:

Gielgud (*sotto voce to Witherby and appreciatively*) Just look at them!
(*Raising his voice*) Such courage! But no glamour. So shabby. Such
flamboyance! Demanding equality? What dreamers they are ...
Witherby The public will only lash out. We mustn't draw attention to
ourselves. It can't be right. I'm sure you could do with some Lyon's
Red label.

No one replies

 Witherby walks away

Terry At least they're fighting for us.
Greg Let's join the march ...
Gielgud Oh, I couldn't. Think of the scandal if anyone saw me.
Greg You'd be a great gay hero — if only you stopped hiding in the
closet and came out on a march.
Gielgud (*shaking his head*) I disgraced you all. I provoked outrage
everywhere.
Greg You and your importuning. First time since Oscar Wilde — you
brought gayness out in the open.
Gielgud An outrage.
Greg If it wasn't for you it would have taken years longer to change
the law.
Gielgud What nonsense! Three quarters of the country was wildly
against me.
Greg But the other quarter won in the end.
Gielgud They'll always hate us and harry us.
Greg Just you wait. Just you see — Terry, let's fall in with them. Let's
show a face.
Terry Sure. It's time to go.

Terry takes Greg in his arms; they are wrapped in an embrace

Greg You give me stars in my eyes.

Terry releases Greg

Terry walks into the open lavatory and vanishes

Greg walks after him

Gielgud I've missed the parade. It's all gone by.
Greg (*a cry of despair*) Terry! Come back!

Witherby appears and sets a tea tray down with two cups of tea and some biscuits

John — he's gone. He's left me again. Help me.

Neither of the men react

Greg walks across the stage and out of sight

The entire set opens up to reveal nothing but a vast open space in the midst of which Gielgud and Witherby sit with the tea things

Witherby Where they gone dashing? They'll miss their tea and biscuits.
Gielgud To join the marchers.
Witherby Well, I live and learn, sir. Tea? Sugar? Milk? Biscuit?
Gielgud Just milk, thank you.

Witherby pours out the tea

A biscuit would be agreeable.

Gielgud and Witherby sit there sipping tea

The sound of the marchers' shouts, cheers and whistles fade out

Witherby Such respectable youngsters. Sad. We won't be seeing them in here again.
Gielgud Yes, the parade's gone by ... When do they close you down?
Witherby End of the week. Then I have to take retirement.
Gielgud Of course. I sympathize.
Witherby D'you have a hobby in your retirement, sir? Something to keep you busy?
Gielgud I do a bit of acting.
Witherby That's nice. Anything fancy? The television, I suppose.
Gielgud Theatre — I'm to play an old queen.
Witherby That's a dare. Yes. I see all the musicals. I loved the old music-hall star. Now Marie Lloyd ——

Gielgud "If you show the boys just a little bit, it's a little bit that the boys admire." I've always remembered that.

Witherby Those were the days. I was wondering — have you a special someone?

Gielgud Oh, I've someone at home. There was a young man in the nineteen fifties, but you know ——

Witherby Ah yes ——

Gielgud And you?

Witherby No. No. I was passed over.

Gielgud You live and learn.

Brian's voice (*recorded*; *singing*)

> I was just a seeker after love, you know.
> I thought of aiming high, but always had a longing
>   for the low.
> I tried my luck on summer nights in green and open
>   spaces,
> I cruised in cottages and picked up in the usual bars.
> Now ending up alone I no longer hope for stars.
> I lie awake and dream of better nights, of lost,
>   remembered faces
> Of all those loves I'm only left with traces.

Witherby Perhaps there's someone round the corner.

Gielgud The parade's gone by.

Witherby You can only look back.

Gielgud Strange how the past loses its sting in the end.

CURTAIN

FURNITURE AND PROPERTY LIST

Basic setting throughout the play: Dudmaston Mews Victorian lavatory:

Entrance
Two rows of antique urinals with polished pipes
Victorian washbasins equipped with ancient taps
Cubicles with doors
Glass cisterns
Small cubicle with frosted glass windows (near entrance)

ACT I
Scene 1

Personal: **Bellinger**: torch
Goddard: opulent binoculars

Scene 3

On stage: Two park benches

Personal: **Daniel**: silver flask, matches (in back pocket), cigarette
Terry: cigarette

Scene 4

On stage: Tiny table
Vase of flowers
Two scripts
Chair

Scene 5

On stage: Desk with drawer
Two black boxes to which electrodes are attached (in drawer)
Strap (in drawer)
Screen

SCENE 6

On stage: Pail containing scrubbing brush, Gumption, Ibcol, Duraglit, shoe-
              cleaning brushes, cleaning cloths and mop
Personal: **Greg**: sixpence

SCENE 7

On stage: Two chairs

Off stage: Large bag containing pair of tight jeans and tee shirt

Personal: **Terry**: notebook

SCENE 8

On stage: Props/ furniture for Queen Mab's:
              Glamorous art deco cocktail bar with overhead shutters
              Mirror (behind bar)
              Cocktail-making equipment
              Phone
              Tables
              Chairs
              Steps
              Tray (on bar)
              Witch hazel and cloth (behind bar)

Off stage: Bottle of wine (**Brian**)

Personal: **Chiltern**: handkerchief

SCENE 9

On stage: Three armchairs
              Book
              Glass of sherry
              Button (to summon Witherby)
              Two empty sherry glasses

Off stage: Decanter of sherry (**Witherby**)
              Bottle of champagne (**Witherby**)

SCENE 10

Personal: **Gielgud**: cap

SCENE 11

Personal: **Gielgud**: cigarette, lighter
                 Terry: police identity card, police whistle, notebook, handcuffs

SCENE 12

On stage: Writing desk
                 Grandfather clock
                 Phone

SCENE 13

Off stage: Notes (**Terry**)

SCENE 14

On stage: Evening newspaper vendor stand
                 1953 *Evening Standard* newspapers
                 Placard reading "GIELGUD FINED FOR VICE OFFENCE"

Off stage: Umbrella (**Binkie**)
                 Bag containing spectacles (**Sybil**)

Personal: **Binkie**: wallet containing five pound note

SCENE 15

On stage: Antique desk with drawers. *On it*: period telephone, table-lamp
                 1953 *Evening Standard* newspaper
                 Glass (in bottom drawer of desk)
                 Bottle of whisky (in bottom drawer of desk)

ACT II

SCENE 1

On stage: Two chairs
                 Bottle of wine
                 Glass of wine
                 Glass of alcohol
                 Empty glass

Personal: **Gielgud**: cigarette
                 Binkie: watch

SCENE 2

On stage: Old-fashioned Brownie 127 camera
              Copy of the *Evening Standard*
Personal: **Terry**: watch

SCENE 3

On stage: Props/ furniture for Queen Mab's
              Copy of the *Evening Standard*

Off stage: Copy of the *Spectator* (**Greg**)

SCENE 4

On stage: Dressing-room mirror
              Make-up

SCENE 5

On stage: Desk
              Lectern
              Books
              Beer

Off stage: Doll, papers (**Matthew**)

SCENE 6

On stage: Props/ furniture for Sybil's dressing-room:
              Door
              Dressing-room mirror
              Table
              Two chairs
              Wardrobe

              Plate of two bath buns
              Cloth or tissue for removing greasepaint
              Half bottle of champagne (in wardrobe)
              Two glasses (in wardrobe)

Furniture and Property List

SCENE 7

On stage:	Copy of the *Evening Standard*
	Cup of coffee
	Two chairs
Off stage:	Port, glass of wine, pot of coffee (**Witherby**)

SCENE 8

On stage:	Props/ furniture for Sybil's dressing-room
	Silver coffee jug
	Milk
	Biscuits
	Script (on table)
	Two sandwiches
Personal:	**Gielgud**: black eyepatch
Off stage:	Envelope containing card and newspaper cutting (**Fred**)

SCENE 9

On stage:	Two chairs
	Radio or EP player
Off stage:	Knapsack (**Greg**)

SCENE 10

On stage:	Small table
	Coffee
	Silver flagon of champagne
	Glass
Personal:	**Gielgud**: Turkish cigarette

SCENE 11

On stage:	Desk. *On it*: bottle of wine, two glasses

SCENE 12

On stage:	Props/furniture for Queen Mab's
Personal:	**Daniel**: card

Plague Over England

Scene 13

On stage: Props/ furniture for Dudmaston Mews public lavatory, with
                    alterations:
                    Outlines of urinals is seen in fragmented, dilapidated outline
                    All but one of the cubicle doors swing open

Off stage: Pail of water, cloths and dusters (**Witherby**)
                    Tea tray with two cups of tea, biscuits (**Witherby**)

LIGHTING PLOT

ACT I, SCENE 1

To open: Exterior light, twilight. A dozen tiny illuminations (cigarette lights) flicker around

Cue 1	**Bellinger**: "But it's not a usual practice at all." *Another cigarette light flares*	(Page 2)
Cue 2	Human whistles sound *Cigarette lights are extinguished. Torch lights gleam*	(Page 2)
Cue 3	Police whistles sound *Big lights begin to circle*	(Page 2)
Cue 4	Shouts and cries. More police whistles *A concentration of lights*	(Page 3)

ACT I, SCENE 2

To open: Interior light, day

No cues

ACT I, SCENE 3

To open: Exterior light, night. Lamp light plays on the back projection of the Serpentine

No cues

ACT I, SCENE 4

To open: Interior light, day

No cues

ACT I, Scene 5

To open: Interior light, day

No cues

ACT I, Scene 6

To open: Interior light, evening

No cues

ACT I, Scene 7

To open: Interior light, day

No cues

ACT I, Scene 8

To open: Interior light, early evening

No cues

ACT I, Scene 9

To open: Interior light, early evening

No cues

ACT I, Scene 10

To open: Exterior light, midnight

Cue 5	**Gielgud** walks briskly into the darkness	(Page 36)
	Black-out	

ACT I, Scene 11

To open: Spotlight on **Gielgud**. Beams of light focus on the lavatories

ACT I, Scene 12

To open: Interior light, night

No cues

ACT I, Scene 13

To open: Interior, day

Cue 6	When ready	(Page 43)
	Searchlight begins to beam all round the stage and	
	settles on **Gielgud**	

ACT I, Scene 14

To open: Exterior light, evening

No cues

ACT I, Scene 15

To open: Interior light, evening

Cue 7	**Binkie**: "Good luck."	(Page 49)
	The Lights go down. After a pause, bring up spotlight	
	on **Gielgud**	

ACT II, Scene 1

To open: Interior light, night

No cues

ACT II, Scene 2

To open: Exterior light, late afternoon thin, autumnal sunlight

No cues

ACT II, Scene 3

To open: Interior light, evening

No cues

ACT II, Scene 4

To open: Interior light, evening

| *Cue* 8 | **Binkie**: "... it's not in my mouth." | (Page 60) |
| | *The Lights dim. Spotlight on* **Binkie** | |

| *Cue* 9 | **Binkie** exits | (Page 60) |

Take out spotlight on **Binkie**

| *Cue* 10 | **Gielgud** stands up | (Page 61) |

Spotlight on Gielgud

ACT II, SCENE 5

To open: Interior light, twilight. Light extends to the sofa for a moment, then
                goes out

| *Cue* 11 | **Matthew** and **Fyfe** scrutinize papers | (Page 63) |

Lights come up on **Greg** *and* **Terry**

ACT II, SCENE 6

To open: Interior light

No cues

ACT II, SCENE 7

To open: Interior light, evening

No cues

ACT II, SCENE 8

To open: Interior light

No cues

ACT II, SCENE 9

To open: Interior light

No cues

ACT II, SCENE 10

To open: Exterior light

No cues

ACT II, SCENE 11

To open: Interior light, early evening

No cues

ACT II, SCENE 12

To open: Interior light, evening

Cue 12   **Witherby** and **SM** clear the furniture from   (Page 87)
             Queen Mab's
           Lights flicker and begin to fade and turn to silvery mistiness

Cue 13   **Greg**: "You don't have to tell me."   (Page 88)
           Lighting turns blue

PROJECTION PLOT

ACT I

ACT II

EFFECTS PLOT

ACT I

Cue 14	**Gielgud**: "How stupid I've been." *The phone rings*	(Page 42)
Cue 15	**Gielgud**: "My lavatorial debacle." *The phone rings*	(Page 48)
Cue 16	The Lights go down *A soundtrack of voices, chatter as of the rehearsal* *room, then a hush*	(Page 49)

ACT II

Cue 17	**Chiltern**: "... just a nasty dose of hubris." *The bell rings*	(Page 50)
Cue 18	To open SCENE 4 *Amplified sounds of an audience out front from a* *loudspeaker*	(Page 60)
Cue 19	Spotlight on **Binkie** *Audience sounds fade*	(Page 60)
Cue 20	**Gielgud** and **Sybil** face the audience *A cry or two of "bravo"; a great, enduring outburst of* *applause. Applause resounds, more cries of "bravo",* *then fades*	(Page 61)
Cue 21	The Lights come up on **Terry** and **Greg** *Skeets Macdonald's "Don't Let the Stars Get in Your* *Eyes" plays. It fades in and out for the remainder of* *the scene as the action switches between the two sides* *of the stage*	(Page 63)
Cue 22	To open SCENE 9 *Elvis Presley plays*	(Page 75)
Cue 23	**Greg** turns off the radio *Elvis Presley music cuts out*	(Page 75)
Cue 24	To open SCENE 10 *David Bowie's "Ziggy Stardust" plays, then fades*	(Page 77)
Cue 25	To open SCENE 12 *Porter's "Let's Fall in Love" plays*	(Page 83)
Cue 26	**Greg**: "Now you turn up." *"These Foolish Things" begins to play*	(Page 87)

| *Cue* 27 | The lighting turns blue | (Page 88) |
| | *Brian Eno's "Music for Airports" plays* | |

Cue 28	To open SCENE 13	(Page 88)
	The sound of Evelyn Laye singing "I'll See You Again"	
	comes from Witherby's cubicle	

Cue 29	**Gielgud**: "There's nothing to say"	(Page 90)
	Silence, then "Don't Let The Stars Get In Your Eyes"	
	plays	

| *Cue* 30 | **Terry** and **Greg** stand looking at each other | (Page 92) |
| | *New music: Scott Walker's "No Regrets" plays* | |

| *Cue* 31 | **Greg**: "Yes." | |
| | *Music fades* | |

APPENDIX

Late on 20th October, 1953, Sir John Gielgud, then at the zenith of his fame as one of the great, twentieth-century actors, was arrested in a Chelsea public lavatory. The next morning he pleaded guilty to the charge of persistently importuning for immoral purposes. Gielgud, then directing and acting in N.C. Hunter's *A Day By The Sea*, was fined £10. The magistrate told him to see his doctor at once. Within a few hours the fearful actor found himself front page news in the (London) *Evening Standard*. The next morning every national newspaper gave prominent attention to the story of Gielgud's fall from grace. The actor was caught in the one great emergency of his life.

The press were almost uniformly hostile, seized by the belief that Gielgud's conviction was a symptom of the moral decay infecting Britain. The *Sunday Times* diagnosed a "serious criminal problem" and an "evil that is dangerous and growing." It blamed the country for having lost its sense of moral direction and straying into unwholesome terrain. That weekend John Gordon of the *Sunday Express* vented the fashionable view that homosexuality — "moral rot" as he termed it — was "akin to an infectious disease." "It infects politics, literature, the stage, the Church ..." Gordon wrote. The following Sunday he called for Gielgud to be stripped of the knighthood he had been awarded in the Coronation honours. A petition, to have Sir John stripped of his membership of Equity, the actors' union, was sent round to every West End theatre. This move came to nothing. If successful it would have meant the end of Gielgud's career. David Astor, editor of the *Observer* suitably described some press reaction as being voiced in the language of a witch-hunt.

Not since Oscar Wilde's inexorable fall from glory to ignominy at the Old Bailey nearly sixty years earlier, had such a famous man been up in court on a homosexual charge. In the early 1950s, Britain was swept by waves of moral panic and hysteria, traditional symptoms of the witch-hunt mentality. Homosexuals had come to be regarded as devious proselytizers, disseminators of what was frequently likened to an epidemic, plague and cancer. Normal young men, it was said, were seduced into homosexual acts to which they became ruinously addicted for life. A discreet group of people, identified by their sexual activities, were stigmatized by judges, politicians and doctors as a rather creeping evil that threatened family life and the country's very future.

The intensity of this panic about queers was reflected in court cases all over England. Groups of sexually linked men were rounded up and when found guilty given prison sentences, even where the sexual acts had been committed in private. Judges and magistrates were particularly alarmed by the fact that those who behaved homosexually often crossed the rigidly manned class barriers of the time. It was to be a prime feature of the famous 1954 court case involving the young Lord Montagu, two of his friends, the diplomatic correspondent of the *Daily Mail*, Peter Wildeblood, and Michael Pitt-Rivers, together with two members of the RAF.

In 1953 a succession of public figures, of whom Gielgud was far and away the best-known and most highly regarded, were either convicted of gay offences that year or else a few months later were visited by the police. For understandable but perhaps fanciful reasons some gay men became convinced a campaign was afoot specifically to target well-known homosexuals and make an example of them. A Labour MP was caught importuning at Piccadilly Circus and resigned his seat. The novelist Rupert Croft-Cooke was sent to prison for nine months after being found guilty of sex with two sailors — in his own home. Lord Montagu found himself in court charged with serious offences involving a boy scout. When the jury failed to agree on one of the charges the Director of Public Prosecutions, Sir Theobald Mathew, decided to go for a second trial of Montagu in 1954.

Until Gielgud's fall from grace, though, the word "homosexual" was almost taboo in national newspapers or on radio and television. The *Sunday Pictorial*, edited by Hugh Cudlipp, alone broke the general vow of silence on the subject, by publishing a sensational three-part series on Evil Men (homosexuals that is) in 1952. For that which is repressed almost always comes out in some agitated, indirect or euphemistic form — thanks to the fascination of the forbidden. The mass-circulation *News of the World* had long pandered weekly to the prurience of its readership with enthusiastic, weekly court-reporting of offences involving homosexuality. The words it used to talk about gay offences were always euphemistic. "Serious" and "grave" and "unnatural" were the words used. Judges talked about "vice". Plays about homosexuality or homosexual characters were invariably banned by the Lord Chamberlain, a senior official of the Household who was responsible for stage censorship. Even so, the forbidden subject was vented in plays, novels and even opera with coded references and allusions.

The origins of this outbreak of what now appears institutionalized homophobia today are complex, induced by a combination of post-war political, social, medical and cultural theories.

The historian David K. Johnson, in his revelatory book *The Lavender Scare* (2004), yet to be published in Britain, for the first time exposed the extent to which Republican politicians characterized homosexuals as security risks from 1947, when the Cold War began its rapid freezing activities, and continued to do so with ever-increasing enthusiasm. Historians have, in the past, neglected this specifically gay field of study. "In 1950 many politicians and journalists thought that homosexuals posed more of a threat to national security than communists", Johnson wrote. The real witch-hunt in America was a gay-directed one, more significant than the greatly publicized purge of homosexuals. Hundreds of gay men and some lesbians were arbitrarily removed from all branches of the federal service and the State Department in particular.

To countervailing expressions of disbelief and dismay the Kinsey Report of 1948 claimed that more than a third of American males had behaved homosexually at some time in their lives. The advent of the Cold War had of course put the western powers on heightened alert against a supposedly aggressive and expansionist Russia. Crucially the defection in 1950 to the Soviet Union of two British diplomats, the gay Guy Burgess and the bisexual Donald Maclean, invited and incited an influential conviction that homosexuality, communism and treachery were linked as if by an umbilical cord. President Truman's Democrat administration was harassed by Republican senators as early as 1947. Truman was accused of being complacent about the risk said to be posed by blackmailable homosexuals in the public service. In 1953 the newly-elected President Eisenhower initiated a new security programme for those suspected of disloyalty (communism) or posing a security risk (usually homosexuality). The *Manchester Guardian* reported on 27th October 1953 that in the first four months of the Eisenhower programme 1,456 had left their jobs, either being dismissed or resigning. Britain did not succumb to such anxiety. This did not mean that governments both Labour and Conservative were supine.

The Attlee government introduced a mild version of the Eisenhower security programme in 1948 and the 1951 Churchill administration followed suit with a system of positive vetting. Although a mere 135 English civil servants were named as security risks between 1948 and 1955, there could be no missing the fact that by 1953 homosexuals in the civil service had come to be regarded as inherently unsuited to take on any security-related position. Sir David Eccles, the Conservative Cabinet Minister, half admitted the fact in the House of Commons in 1954.

1953 was the year in which Gielgud's reputation had reached a peak of public glory. On the night after the morning news of his knighthood was published the audience at the Lyric Hammersmith, where he was playing Otway's *Venice Preserv'd*, gave him a standing ovation. That summer when he went to receive his honorary degree at Oxford, Gielgud walked in procession with another honorand, David Maxwell Fyfe, the not very impressive Home Secretary who hated homosexuals. It was Fyfe who is reported to have told Rex Harrison, the husband of his sister Sylvia, that he planned to do away with homosexuality.

Weeks later, at a time when Gielgud was rehearsing *A Day by the Sea*, he went to a dinner party and walked home, stopping off at Dudmaston Mews. Although spiritually scarred for the rest of his life by his conviction, unwittingly he helped break the taboo of silence engulfing homosexuality and gave a human face to the sinister, alien "queer" of the press's imagining. Thanks to Gielgud the unspeakable subject was, therefore, brought out into the open, just weeks before the two trials of Montagu, which rebounded adversely on both the DPP and the police, the second Montagu trial may have led to prison sentences for all three defendants, but the police behaviour — searches of the arrested men's properties without search warrants, the forging of Montagu's passport to make him appear a liar, the pressure placed upon two young RAF men to turn Queen's evidence — caused a backlash against the forces of authority. Fyfe decided Sir John Wolfenden's Committee of Inquiry into Prostitution should consider the problem of homosexuality as well. Wolfenden's mildly liberal report paved the way for campaigners to begin the arduous and lengthy struggle for gay law reform.

Gielgud's tentative flirtation with the avant garde, which had begun when he had come to the support of John Whiting's extraordinary play *Saint's Day*, was abandoned. For the next decade he seemed to lose his theatrical way. For the rest of his long life he never identified himself with any gay cause or organization.

Nicholas de Jongh, October 2009